## Cambridge English Readers

·······················································

### Level 6

Series editor: Philip Prowse

# *Nelson's Dream*

## J. M. Newsome

D1464723

**CAMBRIDGE**
UNIVERSITY PRESS

CAMBRIDGE UNIVERSITY PRESS

Cambridge, New York, Melbourne, Madrid, Cape Town, Singapore,
São Paulo, Delhi, Dubai, Tokyo, Mexico City

Cambridge University Press
The Edinburgh Building, Cambridge CB2 8RU, UK

www.cambridge.org
Information on this title: www.cambridge.org/9780521716048

First published 2008
4th printing 2011

J. M. Newsome has asserted her right to be identified as the Author of the Work in
accordance with the Copyright, Design and Patents Act 1988.

Printed in China by Sheck Wah Tong Printing Press Limited

*A catalogue record of this publication is available from the British Library*

ISBN 978-0-521-71604-8 Paperback
ISBN 978-0-521-71605-5 Book with Audio CDs (3) Pack

# Contents

# Characters

*The story is set in the imaginary African country of Gomokure in 2003.*

**Nelson Mbizi:** a hotel management graduate
**Ruby Mbizi:** Nelson's mother
**Washington Mbizi:** Nelson's father
**Philomena:** Ruby Mbizi's housekeeper
**Melanie Mawadza:** Philomena's neighbour and friend
**Eddy Mawadza:** Melanie's eldest son
**Daniel:** Melanie's second son
**Lily Anne:** Melanie's daughter
**Blessing:** Melanie's baby son
**Viki:** a television presenter
**Phil:** a television cameraman
**Tobias Nakula:** a grocery store owner
**The Chivasa family:** family friends of Daniel's
**Sister Michael:** a nun in charge of Saint John's Hospice
**Mrs Murape:** Washington Mbizi's lawyer
**Kundai Kambera:** a pop star

**Glossary of African words**
[1] **Sadza:** a food made from boiling ground corn
[2] **Jacaranda:** a large tree with blue flowers native to South America often planted in avenues in African cities
[3] **Flamboyant:** a large tree with red flowers, often planted in avenues in African cities
[4] **Combi:** a small minibus used on urban routes
[5] **Mbira:** a musical instrument made from flattened nails held down onto a wooden board by a metal strip, which is therefore cheap to make

# Chapter 1   *Endings*

That Friday evening, at Heathrow Airport, Nelson Mbizi turned to wave a last goodbye to his student friends. They were jumping up and down, making crazy faces and shouting his name. They'd given him a huge soft toy, a bear with the name Paddington written across its blue jacket. He felt stupid carrying it, but didn't know what else to do with it.

'Bye! Thanks for the bear!' he called, lifting the bear up and waving it as he walked through to security. It was sad saying goodbye, but he was glad he'd got his degree and was leaving the greyness of London to go back to sunny Gomokure, his home country.

He stood in the security queue and thought about the people he'd met during his hotel management studies. He was going to miss some of them badly, especially Jackie. There were those who had laughed at him when he told them he wanted to go home to Africa and 'make things better'. But Jackie had said, 'Even if you don't know how yet, I'm sure you'll make a big difference some day.'

Nelson and Jackie had been lovers for a year, but when they both realised they wanted to go home to their own countries, they'd agreed their affair was over. She'd left for Australia two days before. The sadness of missing her was like a gentle ache in Nelson's chest.

Once through security, he bought a cappuccino and sat watching the planes come and go, and the sun go down. He thought of his lovely but difficult mother, and his big, airy bedroom. He thought of his father, who had ridiculed him so often, but still wanted him to work in one of the hotels he owned – a man who never asked people to do things, but just ordered them around. He wasn't going to be the easiest of bosses. 'Still,' thought Nelson, 'it'll be good to be earning my own money.'

The loudspeakers announced Nelson's flight. 'Flight 087 to Kurupenda is now boarding at Gate 53.'

* * *

Kurupenda, the capital city of Gomokure, has many suburbs. Some are luxurious with large houses and gardens. Some, like Chapangana, have narrow, dusty streets and tiny houses. On the same Friday evening, in a small house in Sector D, a crowded area of Chapangana, a sixteen-year-old boy sat beside his mother.

She was quiet today. She lay on the earth floor, wrapped in a blanket with another on top. Once, her skin had been clear and dark like chocolate, but now that she was sick, large parts of her face and arms were white and dry. She was shivering with cold. Her lips were cracked and bleeding, and she was so thin that her bones showed through both blankets. Daniel and his brothers and sister had watched their mother slowly dying for months.

She opened her eyes.

'Daniel,' she said. 'Go and see if Philomena's coming.' Her voice was weak, but her eyes burned in her bony face.

'OK,' he said and smiled at her.

'Don't waste time!' Her voice was deeper than he had ever heard it. 'And ask your sister to come here.'

'OK,' he said again and turned away. Daniel went through the front room where his eldest brother, Eddy, was pretending to be asleep on the bare floor. He went on out into the tiny yard. His sister, Lily Anne, was playing with their baby brother, Blessing, in the dust. She had on her bright pink shoes. 'Mum wants you,' he said.

Lily Anne went in. She knew what to do. All four of the children had been living with this illness for a long time. Their father had died the year before.

Daniel stood in the tiny garden of number 1175, Sector D, looking up the long, straight street. He prayed that Philomena would come quickly. She was the only friend his mother seemed to trust.

He could see people moving, black against the setting sun: groups of teenagers laughing and chatting, smaller children playing and running about, adults coming home from work, tired but cheerful because it was Friday. Music came from the small, boxy houses – radio music, guitar music, traditional songs. Only number 1175 was silent.

Then, among the dark bodies in the shining fog of dust, he saw Philomena, tall, thin and graceful, carrying a large bag on her head. She went into her house, number 1163. Daniel ran to her gate. He called, 'Knock, knock.'

'Come in,' she said as she came to the door. 'Ah, it's you, Daniel. What is it?'

'Mum is sorry to interrupt your evening, but she needs to speak to you. Can you come now?'

Philomena went inside, picked up her keys, closed the door, and followed Daniel without a word.

At number 1175, Daniel took Philomena into the back room. He saw her stop for a second, as usual, to adjust to the smell. Then she smiled her wide smile, sat on the floor by his mother, and picked up a thin, dry hand.

'Melanie,' she said, 'I've come.'

Melanie was too weak to lift her head, but she opened her eyes and tried to smile at her friend. She took a deep breath. 'My time has come,' she said. 'I have to ask you to do one more favour for me.'

'Anything,' promised Philomena.

'I want you to ask your rich employer to help my children … There's nobody else I can turn to.'

'I'll do that,' replied Philomena.

'The older ones are not sick.' Melanie spoke in short bursts. 'Eddy's seventeen and not interested in school … so he's looking for a job. But he won't be able to support the others … Daniel is clever, so he'll need help to finish school … and with his music. Lily Anne should do four more years of school, and she's a good cook … One day she'll be a good housekeeper. There's been almost no money since their father died, but she still feeds us all somehow.'

Daniel watched the tears running out of his mother's eyes and into her strangely white ears. The drops then fell onto the clean white pillow, making a wet mark. Lily Anne stood nearby, waiting for a chance to change the pillow.

Melanie could hardly breathe, but she went on. 'But little Blessing will join me soon. He is sick, like me.'

'Are you sure?' asked Philomena.

'He was born after their father got sick … He was tested with me at the hospital at Christmas.'

'You didn't tell me the result,' said Philomena.

Melanie's hand jumped in Philomena's, and she tightened her grip. 'You *will* do this for me?' she begged, and coughed a terrible, bubbling cough. She took a deep breath and pain showed on her face. Her eyes burned into Philomena's.

Philomena nodded. 'I promise,' she said.

'Ask Eddy and Blessing to come to me,' Melanie said.

Philomena pulled open Melanie's fingers and stood up. She turned and ran through to the front door.

'Eddy, bring Blessing,' she called as she ran. 'At once!'

Eddy was ready. He came in, put Blessing down beside his mother and kissed the top of her head. She lifted her hand to touch Eddy's face. He stepped back and got down on his knees beside Daniel. Lily Anne stood beside them.

'Come, Daniel,' his mother said. Daniel bent over his mother to kiss her head. She wiped a tear from his face with her hard, dry hand. 'When I am free,' she whispered, 'I will always be nearby.'

Daniel smiled as his tears fell on her blankets. 'I will always listen for your voice,' he promised. He went back to kneel by Eddy. He knew someone should say something like they did in church, but he couldn't think what.

Lily Anne went to her mother, kissed her hand and stepped back before she could speak. Little Blessing sat on the earth floor, playing with a leaf he'd picked up outside.

'God, take care of my children,' Melanie cried out in a deep voice like a man's. She gasped and coughed. Her eyes opened wide and went dull. She didn't breathe in again.

The children didn't move.

Philomena crawled forward on her knees. Her tears blinding her, she lifted the hand that was stretched out towards Blessing and laid it on Melanie's chest. She closed Melanie's staring, empty eyes, and sat back.

Eddy jumped up, impatiently wiping his eyes and his nose on the bottom of his T-shirt.

'Is she dead?' he asked Philomena.

'Yes.'

'So now what?' he shouted. 'Now what? What the hell are we supposed to do now?!' He turned and went into the other room. 'What the hell!? What the hell!?' His angry voice filled the little house. Then he ran out into the street.

Lily Anne took Blessing in her arms and lifted him up, her young face expressionless. 'I only have enough sadza[1] for us to eat today and tomorrow,' she said to Philomena.

'I've got some,' said Philomena, her eyes on her dear friend's peaceful face. 'You'll eat with me tonight.'

Daniel got up from his knees and sat beside his mother, touching her hair. He whispered to her, 'We talked about it, but we didn't really believe it … You weren't supposed to really die. Nobody will love us like you did.' The last orange light of the sun shone through the little window and gently touched his mother's cheek.

Daniel heard Philomena go out to find someone to help with the body. The women in the street began the loud weeping he had heard so often lately. He stood up and walked outside in a dream. Life would be very different from now on.

# Chapter 2 *Home again*

Early on Saturday morning, Nelson stood waiting for his suitcases at Kurupenda Airport. In the three years since he'd left, a shiny new airport had been built. As he looked around, he saw his mother waving from behind a glass wall. He smiled and waved back. She had on a long red and white dress and a head cloth, and she was laughing.

'You look wonderful, Mum,' he said as they met. He hugged her and lifted her off her feet.

'You look too much like an adult!' she replied. 'Put me down! Where is my little boy?'

'Not there any more, Mum. I'm twenty-two now. I've even got a real job, if Dad still wants me to work for him.'

'Oh, he does. He's been talking about it for weeks now. Is this toy bear yours?'

'Yeah. My friends gave him to me to "look after" me!'

Ruby Mbizi laughed and took Nelson's arm. 'Now you're home you'll be well looked after!' She led him out to a new Mercedes that shone in the early-morning sun.

As Nelson and his mother drove towards their house, Nelson looked out for things he remembered. The jacaranda[2] trees were flowering the same misty September blue in the avenues. Most of the buildings were the same, some modern with a lot of glass, some older, and some like buildings he'd seen in London.

At last they were driving up their own leafy street. The great white gate was still the same, but it opened electronically now. The man in the little gatehouse was new. He touched his hat and called out, 'Good morning, Mrs Mbizi, young Mr Mbizi!' as Nelson's mother drove into their garden.

Nelson saw that the bushes round the tennis court were taller and the house had been painted a paler pink than he remembered. But the great spreading flamboyant[3] tree by the swimming pool hadn't changed, the perfectly cut grass was still as richly green, and the flowerbeds were even more colourful.

'It's good to be home,' he said as they went up the steps into the house.

'Are you hungry?' his mother asked.

'You bet!'

'I'll ask Cook to make you some breakfast. Come into my sitting room. There's something I want to show you.'

Ruby Mbizi sat down at her desk and pulled a large photograph towards her.

'Your second cousins,' she said with a smile.

Three lovely young women were sitting on the deck of a luxurious river boat. They all wore bikinis and had the same empty smile on their perfect faces.

'Look, Mum ...' Nelson was embarrassed by what he knew was coming. He walked over to the window.

Ruby smiled. 'You'll need some company, and they're all in town just now. You have a choice of three!'

'Let's leave it a week or two, shall we, Mum?'

There was a knock on the door and Mrs Mbizi called out, 'What is it?'

Philomena, the housekeeper, came in. 'Excuse me, madam, but can I ask you something?'

Nelson turned from the window to look at Philomena.

'Oh, I'm sorry, Mr Nelson.' Philomena's smile was like a light in the dark by the door. 'Welcome back. I didn't know you were here.'

'Thank you, Philomena,' Nelson said. 'Good to see you.'

'I'll come back later, madam.' Philomena turned to go.

'Was it something private?' asked Ruby Mbizi.

'Not really, madam. But it's important. I wanted to ask you for help for some children. They've just lost their mother and their father and they're orphans now.'

Nelson saw his mother's face harden.

'Well, Philomena, if I helped every child in that situation I would have nothing left within a week, isn't that so?' Mrs Mbizi said with a false little smile.

'That's true, madam.' Philomena looked down at her shoes. Nelson turned back to the window. 'It was the mother's dying wish that I asked you,' she said.

'Well, now you have. Is there anything else?'

'No, madam.'

'That's all then, Philomena. Thank you.'

Nelson waited until the door had closed and then asked his mother, 'Couldn't you give something to the church and ask them to help that family? Then you needn't say the money's from you and you won't have others begging ...'

'Nelson, my dearest, there are now thousands and thousands of AIDS orphans in this country. There's nothing anyone can do about it.'

'There must be, Mum. There must be organisations ...'

'Well, I'm not an organisation.'

'Perhaps Philomena just doesn't know who to ask.'

'Well, nor do I. So there's an end to it.'

13

Nelson was tired. He hadn't slept much on the plane and he knew he would never persuade his mother to think about something when she didn't want to.

'How's Dad?' he asked.

'Busier than ever. I hardly ever see him.' Ruby smiled a twisted smile and her eyes warned him off the subject.

'I'll go and have some breakfast by the pool,' he said.

Nelson bent to kiss her and went to the kitchen, leaving Ruby looking at the photograph.

The smell of Cook's biscuits and the warmth from the oven met him in the corridor. He stopped just before the kitchen as he heard Philomena say his name.

'You didn't tell me Mr Nelson was back,' she was saying.

'No. I thought you'd get a nice surprise,' said Cook.

'What do you mean by that?'

'Well, he's always been your favourite.'

'He's everybody's favourite, not just mine. He's much too nice to have Mr and Mrs Mbizi as parents.' Cook and Philomena laughed. This seemed to be an old joke. Nelson coughed to warn them he was coming.

Cook said loudly, 'Is Mr Nelson's orange juice ready?'

'Hello, Cook,' said Nelson as he came into the kitchen. 'I do believe you've got a bit fatter!'

Cook laughed with delight and clapped her hands.

'You sound very English now, Mr Nelson,' said Cook.

Nelson smiled. 'Philomena, can you bring my breakfast out to the pool?' he asked.

'Of course,' she said.

Nelson was almost asleep in the early sun when she arrived with a heavy tray. She put the tray down on a small table beside Nelson and turned to go.

'Philomena.' Nelson sat up and looked at the glass of orange juice. 'What's the name of the family of orphans?'

'The mother was Melanie Mawadza. There are four children.'

'What's their address?' He focused on his plate.

'Number 1175, Sector D.'

'Mmm. Do you live near there?'

'Yes. Five houses further up.'

'Do they have any money at all?' Nelson was still looking down, careful not to look into Philomena's eyes, remembering his African manners.

'I think they own their house and they may be OK for a short while. But nobody is earning just now.'

'OK, Philomena. Thanks.' He looked up at last.

'Thank you, Mr Nelson.' Philomena turned and left.

'Why did I ask her about those children?' he thought as he ate. 'I can't do anything to help. I've got no money.' His parents had always talked of life in the Sectors as ugly and dangerous and had forbidden him to go there. 'Forget it,' he thought. 'Better not to get involved.'

# Chapter 3 *Sector D*

Nelson didn't see his father that first evening. Mr Mbizi was the government Minister for International Trade as well as a hotelier, and he was giving a speech in Parliament.

Next morning, breakfast was laid out as usual under the tree beside the glass doors from the dining room. Nelson sighed happily and sat down. It was good to be back. There was no sign of his mother or his father. But there was a note on the table.

*Welcome home! Sorry to miss you again. I have to be at Parliament again today, so I won't be able to call you. Meet me at the hotel at 5 p.m. I'll introduce you to everyone and you'll start work with Fletcher, the accountant, tomorrow. You've got a lot to learn and I want you to learn it fast. Dad*

'Yuck!' thought Nelson. 'Accounts are not my thing. Perhaps I can get out of that soon and into guest services.'

He called a few friends as he ate, hoping to find a partner to play tennis. But it turned out that none of his old friends was free. They were either busy or out of the country. As he ate the last piece of toast, he was surprised to find himself thinking about Sector D.

His parents would probably be furious if they knew he was even interested, so he'd have to be careful. And without money he wasn't sure there was anything he could do to help. 'But I'd just like to see what it's like,' he told himself.

He went up to his room and put some old clothes into a backpack. Then he borrowed the gardener's truck and drove to a supermarket. In the men's toilets he changed into the old clothes and a woollen hat with a hole in.

Then he joined the queue for a bus. Nobody looked at him and he found he was enjoying being someone else.

In the tiny combi[4] bus the passengers were squeezed together. The girl on Nelson's left was pressed against him. She was pretty and he thought of speaking to her, but the driver had music on so loud there was no point in trying.

Nelson fought his way out of the bus at the Sector D stop. He asked for directions and set off down the long, dusty street. Number 1175 was deserted, the door shut. Nelson was surprised. As it was Sunday, he had expected there to be lots of people around, but in fact the whole area was strangely empty.

Further down the street a great jacaranda tree threw a cool shadow. He walked towards it, enjoying the difference between its blue and the blue of the sky. There was a silent crowd of people in its shade. He moved towards them quietly, keeping close to a fence. As he got nearer he could hear someone singing. The music was from an mbira[5] and the voice was clear and sweet.

Over the heads of the crowd Nelson saw a young man sitting on a rock under the tree. He was playing the mbira and singing. The people around him were moving silently to the music. Some of them were crying.

The young man sang:
*So sit with us and drink a beer.*
*Sit with us and share a tear.*

Nelson saw a man with a television camera in the crowd. The camera was pointed at the singer and sometimes it turned slowly towards the listeners.

17

The young man went on:

*She's left us, but she's still here.*
*Gonna live! Keep her dear.*
*Gonna sing! Hold her near.*
*She's left us, but she's still here.*

When he stopped, the crowd stood still for a moment. Then they all sighed. Some clapped their hands and some just turned away sadly and left.

Nelson stayed back and watched. He saw a girl of eleven or twelve in an old dress and bright pink shoes sitting beside a baby. She got up and started towards the singer.

But the cameraman said, 'Please, Lily Anne. Stay and play with Blessing. I want a shot of you both.'

Behind him, Nelson heard a woman's voice say, 'And then come and get some shots of their house. We'll go to the grave when the light's better. It's too bright just now.'

The young man who'd been singing stood up. He was tall, but much too thin, like a very young tree. He walked past Nelson to cross the road.

'And Daniel,' said the voice, 'you can sing another song at the graveside.'

Daniel went up to a young woman who was standing in the shadow of a tall fence. His hands were tightly closed as he looked down at her, but he spoke quietly. 'I can't sing at the grave. I can only cry there.' And he walked away.

The young woman had a notebook in her hand. She seemed angry as she crossed something out on the page.

'Phil!' she shouted, still looking down at her notes.

The cameraman turned. 'Yeah?' he said. Nelson could see that Phil didn't like his colleague much.

18

She looked up and called out, 'Get those kids over to the house and let's have some shots by the front door.'

Then she turned her head a little and looked in Nelson's direction. He could see straight into her eyes. They were green, and bright with anger. They were the most beautiful eyes he had ever seen. His legs turned to water. He stepped backwards, glad there was a fence behind him.

He couldn't move. It was as if she had pinned him to the fence. But she looked straight through him and stepped out of the shadow. Nelson saw that her skin was the colour of coffee with cream. She walked fast across the road towards number 1175, stepping over a dirty plastic bag like a dancer.

The thinning crowd followed Phil and the young woman. Nelson followed too, once his legs felt stronger.

'Keep back, there,' the young woman shouted. People stepped back, raising white dust in the road. The sun was high now, and very hot.

'You, Lily Anne, show me where your mother was when she died.' The woman and the girl went into the house. Daniel and some friends sat down by the door.

Nelson stayed out in the road, but next to the garden fence. A friend asked Daniel, 'Any news of Eddy?'

'Not yet. He'll come back soon. You know him – it takes a lot of beer and girls to get over the bad times.'

'I saw him yesterday,' said an older man. 'He was at a bottle store in the city centre. He had a girl on each side and a bottle in his hand.'

They all laughed. Daniel played quietly on his mbira while they talked. Phil stood impatiently in the sun.

'Hey, Viki,' he called. 'You ready for me in there?' He'd taken a floodlight and battery out of a black case.

Viki's angry voice called back. 'Yeah. Yeah. OK. Come on in, and bring Daniel.'

Nelson waited against the fence. Daniel took the heavy battery from Phil and went in. Some of the young men began telling each other stories of Eddy's adventures when his father died. They laughed so much they had to sit down in the dust. Nelson had forgotten that most people in his country laughed a lot, and sang, and played music, however bad they were feeling. He found he was smiling too.

Then Viki and the children came out. 'Phil!' she called.

Phil tripped in the doorway and bumped into Viki. 'Keep your big feet away from me!' she said crossly.

Nelson could not take his eyes off her. He wanted to go up to her and say, 'It's OK. Don't be angry. Relax.' Instead he bent over the fence and asked Phil, 'Where are you from?'

Phil was looking down, adjusting the camera. 'South Africa. Network 10. Jo'burg.'

'Right.' Johannesburg was over a thousand kilometres away. So there wasn't much chance of his meeting Viki again. Nelson felt suddenly depressed. He looked around at all the smiling young faces. Everyone was thin and bony, and he could smell rubbish and worse in the street. 'How many of you will be dead soon?' he thought.

Viki was ready for Phil to film her talking. 'Right, let's get on with it,' she said.

Phil was arranging the floodlight on the ground. 'I need this light. Sun's too high. Can't see your face.'

'Oh, for God's sake,' said Viki. 'Just get yourself together, will you!'

Nelson opened his mouth to speak, but Daniel laughed and said, 'Bike up a hill, that's our Phil!' Everyone but Viki laughed.

'Ready,' said Phil with a grin. He switched the light on and turned it towards her.

She stood with her head up and looked directly at Phil's camera. She spoke clearly and with feeling.

'This is the home of Daniel Mawadza and his brothers and sister. They are all under eighteen. Their father died last year. He was thirty-eight. Their mother died two days ago, so they are now orphans. The illness that killed their parents was AIDS. They want me to tell you about it.

'If they'd known what was wrong earlier, maybe their parents could have found treatment. If people could accept that this illness must not be hidden away, then they could talk about it more easily. Daniel and his family have nothing and no-one. They are facing a long, slow death from being poor, if not from being sick, like their parents.

'This is happening all over Africa. Why are the governments of our countries doing so little? I'll tell you why. Because they're frightened by this illness. Because you can get this infection from sex. There'd be no children without sex, and yet, in African cultures, men and women don't talk to each other about it. But because our leaders feel fear and shame, thousands of people die every week, thousands of new graves appear, thousands of families are left without income, thousands of children are orphaned.

'We *must* make sure our governments, our churches and our society as a whole stop thinking of this illness as an illness of shame. We must make sure that everyone knows about it and knows how to stop it. We must make sure that there are fewer families like Daniel's, not more.

'Daniel Mawadza doesn't want to talk on camera. He says that when bad things happen he makes them into music. He plays mbira and sings. Listen to him now ...'

Viki's voice changed completely as she said to Phil, 'Cut that in before the shots of Daniel singing under the tree.'

'Right,' said Phil.

There was a moment of quiet when they finished. Then all the young people began to clap. Viki looked surprised. 'That's enough,' she said and picked up her bag and papers. 'I'll see you at the grave about four thirty, Daniel. Bring Lily Anne and Blessing. See you in the car, Phil.' She walked fast up the street and turned a corner.

Nelson nodded to Phil and then found himself walking after Viki. 'Mistake!' he told himself. 'This is not what you came for. Those kids are going to need help very soon and you have nothing to offer. And that girl's bad news – *and* she lives a thousand kilometres away. Forget her.'

Viki had disappeared. 'Good thing,' Nelson said to himself as he waited for the bus at the top of the street. He felt shocked and sickened by the way these people lived, in spite of their cheerfulness. And he felt helpless. There was nothing he could do to help so many. Nelson thought about his mother's point of view. Better to forget about Sector D and start working at the hotel. At least the hotels provided jobs for some people.

# Chapter 4 *Beginnings*

Nelson's taxi drew up at the steps of the Lion Hills Hotel at four fifty-six that afternoon. Nelson went in through the tall glass doors. At the reception desk a middle-aged man looked up and said, 'Can I help you, sir?'

'I have an appointment with Mr Washington Mbizi at five o'clock,' said Nelson with a polite smile.

'Ah, you must be Nelson Mbizi.' The man grinned.

'And you must be Fletcher.'

'That's right. I'm the accountant. Mr Mbizi told me to wait for you. Good to meet you at last.'

'Pleased to meet you, Fletcher.' They shook hands. 'It's good to be here.' Nelson looked around.

'Your father,' said Fletcher, 'wants us to go straight down to the accounts department and he'll join us there.'

They went down to the basement in the lift. Nelson's father met them there. He looked older and fatter than Nelson remembered, but he seemed genuinely pleased to see his son at last. He took Nelson round and introduced him to what seemed like a hundred people. He showed Nelson some of the hotel rooms, the kitchens, the laundry, the stores and the front office. Later, Nelson and Fletcher sat in the little grey accounts office and Fletcher explained how the flow of money was controlled and recorded.

Nelson wasn't very interested, although he surprised himself by how well he understood. By ten o'clock he was yawning and he went home exhausted, wondering whether managing hotels would be all accounts and no people.

Later that night, in his dreams, Nelson watched Viki from a hilltop. She was by a river, picking flowers. He couldn't move, but he could see beyond the mountains huge black clouds pouring rain. The river was rising, but Viki didn't seem to realise. Nelson called to her, but she couldn't hear him. He tried to go to her, but his feet were attached to the rock. He watched her as the river rose higher and higher. Then suddenly it caught her and she was swept away, screaming for help. Nelson woke with a jump and found he was sweating and shouting her name.

It was morning. He sat up and took a deep breath. The dream faded fast. He managed to forget about it altogether as he showered. Then he went to work, his first adult job.

\* \* \*

When Daniel got home from school on the fifth day after his mother's death, he found Eddy sitting on the step.

'Hey,' he said with a big smile. 'You OK?'

'Better now,' Eddy answered.

Daniel sat down beside Eddy and they both looked at the road. 'Where have you been?'

'Can't remember it all.' Eddy laughed and Daniel joined in. 'But I got a job at that garage in Sector C, like we said.'

'Hey, that's cool,' said Daniel.

'I have to live there.' Eddy looked uncomfortable. 'They won't pay me any money, just food and a bed.'

Daniel picked up a small stone. 'When are you going?'

'Tonight, so I'm there for work tomorrow.'

'Does Lily Anne know?' asked Daniel.

'She's packing my things.'

'When will we see you?'

'Maybe once a week, or …' Eddy hesitated. 'If you need me I'll come.'

'Right.' Daniel threw the stone up and caught it.

'You're the boss here now.' Eddy was almost in tears.

'Yeah. Except Lily Anne's the boss really …' They both laughed again, and the moment passed.

Two friends of Eddy's were walking by and saw him. They came into the garden and shook his hand and hugged him, laughing and joking.

Daniel stood up, unfolding his long legs. He went and got his mbira and sang as the laughter got louder:

*You have no heart, they say.*
*You ran away, they say.*
*With a bottle in your mouth,*
*And a girl round your neck,*
*You didn't even check,*
*Your little brother wasn't crying,*
*While your mother finished dying.*

Some more people came into the garden and stood listening to Daniel. The young men and Eddy stopped playing around.

*Gone five days, they say.*
*Lost your way, they say.*

Lily Anne and Blessing had come out to join the crowd. People were clapping to the music now. Eddy stood among them, listening and pretending the clapping was for him, with a big smile on his face.

*Came home shamed, they say.*
*Can't be blamed, we say.*
*Now I have no mother,*

*It's good you're back, big brother.*
*Welcome home.*

Everyone started to laugh and dance around. 'Welcome home,' they called and sang to Eddy. 'Welcome home.'

\*   \*   \*

For Nelson the days passed quickly as he learned about the hotel. His father had his own way of doing things, so he had to 'unlearn' much of what he'd studied. Fletcher kept an eye on him and reported to Mr Mbizi every day.

A week after he'd started, Nelson found his father at the breakfast table.

'Hi, Dad,' he said as he sat down. 'I was wondering when I'd get paid. I'd like to meet up with some friends, start a savings account, all that grown-up stuff. But I can't do anything without an income.'

Mr Mbizi was reading the paper. He looked at Nelson over the top. He didn't smile. 'You'll get paid when I'm convinced you're worth it. It's early days yet. Fletcher will arrange a small advance if you need pocket money.'

Then Mr Mbizi got up, his large stomach almost knocking a plate off the table. 'See you later,' he said.

Nelson was angry. But his father had always been able to make him angry and he decided to be patient a bit longer. He did meet up with some friends one evening and they talked about sport and music. They were enthusiastic about Kundai Kambera, a South African pop star that Nelson hadn't heard of, who was only a year older than they were. They weren't interested in England, and wanted to discuss girlfriends and how to avoid HIV, and of course the price of cars. Nelson didn't feel at home with them.

\*   \*   \*

The next morning, Nelson was at the top of the stairs when he heard his mother and father arguing in their bedroom. When he was a child, he used to hide and listen when they argued. Now he just stood outside their door, hoping those days were over.

His father's voice wasn't very clear, but he seemed to be saying something about 'not my only son'.

Ruby was shouting as she opened the door to leave. 'Well, he may not be your only son, Washington Mbizi, but he's the only one in the eyes of the law. He's the only one with your name. He's the only one with a good education, and he's the only one you can trust.'

She banged the door shut and ran down the stairs. Nelson stepped quickly aside and she didn't see him.

He walked slowly to his room. He knew his father had had girlfriends – everybody knew – and he'd guessed there were other children. But why was this an issue now? And was it anything to do with his father avoiding paying him – did his father want another son to run the hotels?

Mr Mbizi didn't appear at the hotel all day.

\* \* \*

That evening, Ruby came into the little sitting room where Nelson was watching a film on TV.

She sat down and said, 'I want you to take one of your cousins to the movies, instead of sitting here on your own.'

'Oh, Mum. They're just not my type.' Nelson's eyes didn't leave the screen.

'How do you know? You've hardly seen them since you were all tiny. You'd feel a lot better with a girlfriend.' Ruby touched Nelson's arm.

'I feel fine, Mum,' Nelson replied, still watching TV.

'Well, you don't look fine. You hardly ever smile now, and you spend all your time on hotel business,' said Ruby.

'There's a lot to learn,' Nelson said. When his mother didn't reply, he turned to her. 'Mum, what's this business about … about my being … only one of Dad's sons?'

'How did you …? Nelson, you are his only son.'

'Well, yes, with you, Mum. But …'

Ruby stood up. 'You are legally his only son.'

'I know. Don't get upset, Mum. I just wondered …'

Ruby walked to the door and turned. 'I will not rest until you have everything you've worked for, whatever your father is planning.' She went out and closed the door.

Nelson swore quietly. He wasn't even sure he wanted to spend his whole life in hotels. He already found the constant demands of guests with too much money and a high opinion of themselves very tiring. He might not want 'everything he had worked for'. Why couldn't his parents just tell him what was going on? He was an adult now.

He gave up trying to watch the film and started changing channels to see what else was on.

As the pictures flashed on and off, he heard the name Daniel. He went back a station. Viki's beautiful eyes were looking straight at him and she was saying, 'Daniel Mawadza doesn't want to talk on camera. He says that when bad things happen he makes them into music. He plays mbira and sings. Listen to him now …'

And there was Daniel sitting under the jacaranda tree singing to the small crowd.

# Chapter 5 *Face to face*

Nelson's heart began to beat like a drum. His breath was shaky and he found he was grinning from ear to ear. He jumped up and ran out into the dark garden. He tore off his clothes and dived into the swimming pool. He swam up and down for a long time, until he was calm enough to think. At last he knew what he wanted to do. He needed information – and money.

Next morning, Nelson was in the restaurant with the manager planning a dinner for two hundred when he got a message. His father wanted to see him in his office.

Nelson came out of the lift and saw his father through the door, talking on the phone. Mr Mbizi was bent over, talking very quietly for once. Nelson stood in the doorway until his father saw him and gestured him to come in and sit down. Washington Mbizi's face was grey when he put down the phone, but his voice was as loud as ever.

'So, what do you think of that restaurant manager? Is he doing a good job?' he asked Nelson.

Nelson thought for a moment. 'He doesn't know a lot about the latest fashions in menus, but he's excellent at organising,' he said.

'I was thinking of taking on a new man – younger.'

'It's not my decision,' said Nelson, 'but I wouldn't start someone completely new as the manager, maybe as an assistant at first.' Nelson was looking carefully at his father, waiting for his opportunity.

'Right. I'll think about it. OK. That's all I wanted.'

Nelson stayed in his chair. 'Will you be at Parliament tomorrow?'

'I'm going there now,' Mr Mbizi said.

'Is your import-export bill going through?'

'Not yet. It's scheduled for next week, but there's a lot of opposition.'

Nelson took a breath. 'Dad, what can you tell me about the Health Ministry's AIDS programmes?'

His father's eyes suddenly focused on Nelson's face. 'You positive, then?' he asked roughly.

'No. No. I'm fine. I had a test in the UK and ...' Nelson remembered his father's supposed adventures away from home. 'I'm ... careful. But it seems there's not much money being spent on clinics and social awareness for AIDS. Why's that?'

'Some ministries have budget cuts.' His father turned his attention to collecting papers from his desk.

'But how can the government cut the health budget when so many are in danger?' asked Nelson.

'Politics can be a dirty business,' his father growled.

'So what happens to the money they cut from the health budget?' Nelson couldn't believe what his father was hinting at. Was someone stealing public money?

'Don't ask. I'm just grateful that so far I haven't had any cuts in my ministry. I've got to go.' Mr Mbizi stood up and came round from behind the desk. Nelson stood too. 'What do you care, anyway?' his father asked.

'There's something else I wanted to ask you, Dad.'

'Get on with it then. I'm going to be late at Parliament.'

'It's about what you and Mum said the other day about ... other sons. Have you ... Have I got brothers?'

'Not now, Nelson.' Mr Mbizi was getting angry.

'I asked Mum and she said I'm the only legal son. Why is she worried about that?'

'I don't have time for this now! What does she know anyway? Forget it, Nelson, and concentrate on your work. You still need to take more responsibility for financial decisions and for checking things are done properly.'

'In that case, Dad, I think I deserve a proper salary.'

'Do you even know how the wine cellar is run?' Mr Mbizi's voice was rising. 'Do you have any idea of the costs of the laundry? No, you don't. When you do, we'll talk about real money.'

'Dad, you know those are things I can learn in a few minutes. Why don't you want to pay me properly?'

Mr Mbizi turned and stood in front of Nelson, chin to chin. 'In my eyes, you still have to prove you're worth it!' he said. The whites of his eyes had thick red veins in them.

Nelson tried a different technique. 'You see, Dad, there's a reason I need some real money now. There's a family of kids I've met. They've lost both their parents.'

'Which family?' barked Mr Mbizi.

'They live in … Sector D, Dad. They …'

His father made a sudden movement and punched Nelson in the face. 'What do you know about Sector D? What the hell have you been doing?' screamed Mr Mbizi.

Nelson fell back a step. He put a hand to his lips and felt the blood. His father moved again and Nelson stepped further back. He tripped on a chair and almost fell. Two men from the next-door office came in and grabbed Mr Mbizi's arms as he prepared to hit Nelson again.

Nelson was shaking. He'd forgotten what this was like and the shock that it used to give him. Part of him wanted to hit his father again and again, and part of him wanted to cry like a baby.

His father was fighting to get away from the two men. Nelson looked at him, took a deep breath and said, 'If you want to talk to me about … any of this, I'll be at home this evening.' And he turned and walked carefully to the lift.

He went into an empty guest room to clean his face and take some deep breaths. The news would be all over the hotel by now, and his father would have left for the Houses of Parliament. Nelson decided not to do anything until he'd calmed down. He went back to work.

* * *

That evening in Sector D, Eddy had time off from the garage and came home for the evening. He brought some sadza, so they had something to eat. Lily Anne, Blessing and Daniel had had nothing to eat for nearly three days.

'Why didn't you tell me you had no food?' Eddy asked Lily Anne.

'No money for the phone,' she said, as she put the plates in the bucket to take to the tap in the street to wash.

Eddy swore and looked at Daniel.

'We gotta do something, Dan,' he said.

Daniel looked at him with angry tears in his eyes. 'We've got no money, Eddy. I can't look for work because I have nothing to make phone calls with, or to pay for the combi to go looking. I don't know who can help us now. Philomena doesn't come home till Friday and it's only Wednesday. The only people I know who might are my friend Givemore's parents. But they've got ten kids living in their house now.' He couldn't even try to make up a song, he felt so exhausted.

In the dark outside, they heard a sound. And then a voice called out, 'Knock, knock!'

Lily Anne sat down suddenly. It was Tobias Nakula, the owner of the grocery store on their street.

Eddy opened the door and asked Mr Nakula in. He was short, almost fat, with round cheeks and a smooth voice.

'Boys,' Mr Nakula began, smiling broadly in the candle-light. 'Boys, did Lily Anne tell you I had a word with her today?' Daniel looked at Lily Anne. She nodded slightly, looking at the bucket. Mr Nakula went on, 'And I realise things are very bad for you.'

'We're fine, thank you, Mr Nakula,' said Eddy.

'Of course. But you see, I heard of someone who wants to rent a house in this area. And I thought that might be useful to you. If you could each find somewhere else to live, then you could rent out your house and pay for your food and schooling.'

Eddy and Daniel glanced at each other.

'Who is this someone, Mr Nakula? Shall I telephone him?' asked Eddy.

'No need, Eddy. I'll make the arrangements, if you agree.'

Daniel moved to open the door and spoke quietly. 'That's very good of you, Mr Nakula. We'll drop in to the shop in the morning if we decide that's what we want.'

'Right. OK. Well, children. Think carefully. If you do decide, my mother and my brother and I would be happy to give Lily Anne somewhere to sleep and some food each day. She could even go to school again.'

'Where I go, Blessing goes,' said Lily Anne suddenly.

'Ah ... well.' Mr Nakula sounded confused. 'I'd have to discuss that with Mother, but I think it'd be possible.'

'Thank you, Mr Nakula,' said Eddy, showing him out.

In case Mr Nakula was waiting to overhear their conversation outside, Eddy whispered, 'I'd feel a lot better knowing you all had enough to eat.'

Daniel whispered back, 'If Mrs Nakula will take Blessing as well as Lily Anne, I reckon I could persuade Givemore's mum to let me sleep on their floor.'

'I don't trust that man,' said Lily Anne.

'But imagine living at the grocery store!' said Daniel, and sang quietly:

*'Don't trust that man,' says Lily Anne,*
*But she'll get fat on cho-co-late,*
*And steak and cake and jam.'*

'Yeah!' said Eddy, forgetting to whisper. 'You guys'll be bringing *me* food soon.'

And so the decision was made.

Lily Anne waited till they were all asleep, dug up her last lucky coin from the earth floor in the corner, and slipped out of the house into the ink-black night.

# Chapter 6  *New homes*

Nelson knew he was dreaming because the dried-up gardens he was walking through were the gardens at his home. He could hear Daniel singing in the distance. He seemed to float towards the song and found Daniel standing in the bottom of the empty swimming pool with dead leaves blowing around his feet. There were huge birds in the sky above, birds that eat dead animals. But they began to fly down and sit around the edge of the swimming pool, listening. The song was sweet, but heavy with sadness.

Nelson woke up. Had he heard the phone ringing? If he had, it had stopped now. It was two o'clock in the morning.

The first thing he thought of as he lay awake was the fight with his father. Mr Mbizi hadn't appeared all evening and there'd been no messages. The next thing he thought of was his anger with himself because he hadn't stopped thinking of Viki. Was he trying to help the children because that might result in his seeing her again? Was that the only reason he cared about them?

'No, of course not,' he answered himself. He'd been worried about them before he knew she existed. But his mind went on turning over all the issues of the day before. At last he made a decision and finally slept a little.

In the morning he went to the hotel early. He told Fletcher and the department managers that he was going to take a day off the next day. He'd brought his laptop with him to his tiny office. He got onto the Internet and began a search for organisations that helped people with HIV and AIDS in Gomokure. He was looking for something that covered the Sectors, but he'd found nothing relevant when his desk phone rang.

'You asked me to let you know when your father came in,' said Fletcher. 'He's in his office now.'

'Thanks, Fletcher. Can you meet me there?'

Nelson's heart was hammering as he went up in the lift.

'Good morning, Dad. Fletcher,' he said from the door.

'What's all this about?' said Mr Mbizi loudly.

'Dad, I've decided that if I'm to be the manager of your hotels, so that you can deal with your government business properly, then I deserve a decent salary. I want you to know that I'm going to go downstairs and arrange with Fletcher to put me on the books as an official employee of your company at a suitable rate, and pay my first wages. I didn't want to do this behind your back. That's all.'

Washington Mbizi's mouth was open in astonishment. Fletcher looked from one to the other in fear, waiting for the explosion. Nelson thought his father might get violent again, so he stayed near the door. No-one spoke.

'I'll see you in the basement, Fletcher,' said Nelson after a long moment, and turned to go. As he did, he was puzzled to see his father smiling a small, surprised smile. Nelson took the stairs down so as not to wait for the lift.

Nelson worked until almost midnight, but he didn't see his father again that day.

\* \* \*

The next morning he borrowed the gardener's truck again and drove to the bank. He spent most of the morning opening a personal bank account and making some enquiries about accounts for charities. Then he drove to Sector D. This time he went as himself.

But number 1175 seemed different. There were now two new chairs and a wooden table in the front yard and a strange woman went into the door as he approached. Nelson drove on and parked under the jacaranda tree where Daniel had sung, worried by this development.

It was lunch time, so there weren't many people around. But as he got out of the truck, a silent crowd of children and young people appeared and watched him.

'Can anyone tell me where the Mawadza children are?' he asked.

'Daniel lives at number 1210 now,' answered a young woman with a baby on her back. 'It's in the next street, down nearer the river. He's at school this morning.'

'And Lily Anne and Blessing?'

The woman smiled. 'They're lucky. They've gone to live with the Nakulas. They have the grocery store on the corner.'

'Are they a family? What are they like?' asked Nelson.

'It's two brothers and their mother. They're OK as long as your credit's good!' she said with a little laugh.

'And ... er ... what's his name? The eldest one?'

'Eddy,' replied the young woman. 'He's got a job with bed and food in Sector C.'

'Why did they split up?' Nelson had to ask, although he could guess the answer.

'They ran out of money, so Tobias Nakula arranged for them to rent out their house. He's going to send Lily Anne to school again.'

'That's good,' said Nelson. 'What time does Daniel come home from school?'

One of the boys was older than the others. He stepped forward and said to Nelson, 'He'll be back by now. I can show you where he lives if you like.'

'What's your name?' asked Nelson.

'Henry,' replied the boy, looking at the ground.

'Come on then, Henry. Let's go and find Daniel.' Henry's face split open in a wide grin as he got into the truck with Nelson. They drove off in a cloud of dust, and all the other children looked after them with envy.

\* \* \*

Daniel stood outside his friend Givemore Chivasa's house. He looked at the bright flowers in the tidy little yard and smelled the food cooking. He thought how lucky he was to be here. Mrs Chivasa called to him as he went in.

'Food's on the table, Daniel. Where's Givemore?'

'He's coming. He's chatting with some friends.'

'Girlfriends, I imagine,' laughed Mrs Chivasa.

'Hmm … It smells really good.' Daniel sat down to eat. Three other children were there already and they made a lot of noise joking and laughing at each other.

So Daniel wasn't sure he heard a car door shut until a man's voice called out from the gate, 'Knock, knock!'

'Who's that?' said Mrs Chivasa as she went through to the front door. Daniel heard her say, 'Can I help you?'

'I'm looking for Daniel Mawadza. I'm a friend of his friend Philomena's,' said the voice. It was an educated voice, too educated for Sector D. 'My name's Nelson.'

Mrs Chivasa said 'Ah, of course. I'm Primrose Chivasa. Please come in.'

Daniel had almost finished his food. He stopped eating as Nelson came in. The other children sat suddenly silent.

Nelson was wearing real Levi jeans and a leather jacket, which astonished Daniel. Could Philomena really have friends like this, so good-looking, so wealthy?

'Would you like something to eat?' Mrs Chivasa asked.

'Thank you, but I've eaten.' Nelson smiled, and Mrs Chivasa sat down at the table. Nelson's skin shone black and his teeth were very white in contrast. He sat down opposite Daniel. 'Hello, Daniel. You don't know me, but I know Philomena.'

'Ah ...' Daniel realised who this shining young man must be. 'How is she?'

'She's fine,' said Nelson. 'Hello, everyone,' Nelson said to the other children. They all greeted him shyly, and then sat in silence. Nelson went on, 'I saw you on television, Daniel.'

'We were on TV? Hey, that's great!' Daniel grinned.

'I wondered whether the TV people had come back or been in touch with you again.'

'The reporter woman did say she would talk to people about my singing. But I haven't heard ...'

'Nobody else?' Daniel saw Nelson was disappointed.

'No. But the cameraman, Phil, he left me his card.'

Nelson smiled. 'Ah. And do you still have it?'

'Sure.' Daniel stood up and opened his school bag. 'Are you going to call him?'

'I want to ask what people said about the programme.'

'Well, nobody's said anything to me,' said Daniel. 'Maybe it wasn't showing on our local TV.'

'No, it was on satellite, from Jo'burg, on Sunday.'

Daniel handed Nelson the card and noticed how long and slim and smooth his fingers were.

'Thanks,' said Nelson as he wrote out Phil's number on a piece of paper and put it in his pocket. He gave the card back to Daniel and asked, 'And how are *you*?'

Daniel picked up his mbira. 'I'm just fine, thanks. We're all eating again, and it looks as though there might be money for me and Lily Anne to finish our schooling. And this family is very kind.' He began to play and sing.

*Mama's always singing*
*and Papa's always bringing*
*the money home to feed us.*
*They even say they need us!*

The children all clapped and laughed. Nelson asked, 'Are you both here then, you and your brother?'

'Well, Eddy lives at the garage where he works. He finally came back.' Daniel grinned. 'I made a song about him. Want to hear it?'

'Yeah!' shouted the children.

Nelson laughed. 'Another time, Daniel. What about Lily Anne and Blessing? Are they OK?'

Daniel laughed. 'Yeah. They're in the best place – the grocery store! The only thing they don't have there is the traditional medicine for Blessing.'

'Well,' said Nelson as he stood up. 'That's great. I'd heard from Philomena about your mother's death ...'

Daniel stood up too and interrupted, 'So *your* mother is Mrs Mbizi?'

'That's right,' replied Nelson, looking puzzled.

'Nice woman, your mother.' Daniel made it clear with his voice that he didn't mean it.

'Hey!' said Nelson. 'Don't judge her till you know her.'

'OK. I'll try,' said Daniel with a twisted smile.

Nelson turned to go. 'Thank you, Mrs Chivasa, for taking Daniel into your home. I see you have a lot of other children living with you.'

'It's our pleasure, Mr Mbizi. He's a good boy and he keeps the other children amused.' She gestured for Nelson to go in front of her to the door.

Daniel followed Nelson and Mrs Chivasa. In the front yard, he touched Nelson's arm and looked into his face as he said, 'I've got to say thanks to you. Thanks for coming, thanks for remembering us. Looks to me like your mother gave all her heart to her son when you were born.'

Nelson had to look up a bit to see into Daniel's warm brown eyes. 'She's very loyal to her own,' he said. 'As I'm sure your mother was.'

Daniel felt his eyes suddenly fill with tears. 'Yeah,' he said, looking down. The tears splashed into the dust. 'Anyway, we're all OK for now.'

'I'll let you know if I learn anything from Phil.' Nelson turned to Mrs Chivasa and shook her hand. 'It was good to meet you. Goodbye,' he said.

'Stay well,' said Mrs Chivasa in the traditional way.

Daniel watched Nelson get into a shining dark blue truck and drive away slowly so as not to make too much dust.

Daniel turned to Mrs Chivasa and began to dance her round the garden singing Kundai Kambera's greatest hit 'He's my saviour, I'm his friend'.

\* \* \*

Nelson dropped Henry off and drove back to the main road. He parked in the first place he could find and called Phil's number in Johannesburg from his mobile. It was such a relief to know he could pay the bill himself now. A cheerful voice said, 'Yebo? Phil here.'

'Hi, is that Phil the cameraman?'

'Yeah. Who's this?'

'I'm interested in those people in Sector D in Chapangana. You filmed them a couple of weeks back. The singing guy, Daniel, gave me your number. I'm Nelson.'

'Hi, Nelson,' said Phil. 'How're they getting on?'

'They've run out of money, so they've rented out their house, but that means they've split the family up.'

'That's usually a bad sign.'

'Yeah,' agreed Nelson. 'But they seem to be OK for now. It's just … Daniel has written some more songs, so I wondered if you'd be doing another report on them.'

'There was some talk a couple of days ago about something else in that area, but nothing for sure.'

'Would it be better if I contacted what's her name? The reporter?' Nelson hoped Phil couldn't hear his heartbeat.

'Viki? I doubt it. She's not always very … pleasant and, well, she can be, like, really poisonous at times.'

'Hmm. OK. I'll get in touch with you, then.'

'I'll give you her number, if you like. But don't be surprised if she cuts you off!' Phil gave a small, sad laugh.

'Right. OK. Thanks.' Nelson tried to sound bored as he wrote down the number.

When he hung up, part of him wanted to call Viki immediately. But part of him ridiculed the idea. 'To say what?' he thought. 'And anyway, she's not worth the cost of the call.' Perhaps he'd get an idea about what to say if he checked out the Network 10 website. He drove home too fast.

# Chapter 7  *Rescue*

Late that afternoon, Nelson was in his room researching on the Internet. He had learned everything about Network 10, but nothing more about Viki than he knew already, except her surname. He had started looking again at sites concerning AIDS in Gomokure, when the phone rang and he heard his mother answer it in the hall downstairs.

'Please don't call this number if you want to speak to Philomena.' His mother's voice was raised in anger. There was a pause and then, 'Well, all right this once. But never again,' and a loud, 'Philomena! Where are you?'

Nelson got up and went to the top of the stairs. 'Who is it, Mum?'

'Some kid. Where's Philomena?'

At that moment Philomena came running. 'Sorry, madam,' she said and took the telephone carefully from Ruby. Ruby threw Philomena an angry look and marched off to her sitting room.

Nelson stood at the top of the stairs. What could be so urgent in Philomena's life that meant her friends had broken the rule about phoning?

Philomena put the phone down. Nelson cleared his throat so she would know he was watching.

'Oh, Mr Nelson!' She looked up with frightened eyes. 'Are you busy? Could you give me some advice?'

Nelson ran down the stairs and they both went out into the garden. 'Who was that?' he asked.

'It was Lily Anne. She stole a coin from Mr Nakula to call me again. She's frightened.' Philomena was crying.

'What's happened?' Nelson asked urgently.

'She called me during the night last night to ask me what to do. Oh, God. I should have gone to her ...'

'Just tell me what has happened.'

Philomena stared across the lawn as she said, 'Tobias Nakula and his brother have tried to have sex with her.'

'What?' Nelson felt sick. 'Did they succeed?'

'Lily Anne says she managed to knock over a vase which broke, so their mother Mrs Nakula came in and they left her alone. Now she has to pay for the vase, but she's very afraid to stay, and Blessing won't stop crying.'

'What do you want to do?' Nelson asked.

'I ... I just want to get her out of there.'

'Come on then,' said Nelson. 'Let's just go and get her. We can take her to your house and then decide what to do.'

Philomena looked up at him with sudden hope. 'I'll get my keys,' she said.

The sun was going down as they set off in the gardener's truck.

Nelson drove fast in the failing light. 'I thought the Nakulas were a good family. Everyone was pleased Lily Anne had been so lucky.'

'Yes. We all were. This is hard to believe.' Philomena thought for a while. 'It may be that one or both of the brothers are HIV positive, I suppose. Some men believe that if they are the first to have sex with a girl they'll be cured of HIV.'

'But that's a complete lie!' exclaimed Nelson.

Philomena was quiet. After a while she said, 'I thought of offering them my house when I heard they'd split up. But little Blessing is HIV positive and I'm not sure about the others. If they lived with me, I might get it too.'

'Not if you didn't have sex with them or get some of their blood into your body,' said Nelson quietly.

'Isn't their spit dangerous too?' asked Philomena.

'No. It's only blood and the … er … sex liquids.' Nelson felt himself blushing. Philomena had worked for his mother since he was born, and he felt impolite discussing these things with her, however important they were.

'Ah,' said Philomena.

They drove on in embarrassed silence.

The embarrassment lasted until they were parking outside number 1163, Philomena's house. It was already completely dark and there were no street lights on. There was quiet music coming from somewhere nearby.

Philomena broke the mood. 'You know, Mr Nelson, it's a good thing there wasn't much traffic on the road.'

Nelson laughed nervously. 'You're right. I don't usually drive that fast,' he said.

Philomena unlocked her front door and turned on the light. She began uncovering her kitchen things and arranging for visitors. 'I think it's best if I go alone to start with. I'll say the children are coming to stay with me for now. Then we can decide what to do.'

'Fine,' agreed Nelson. 'I'll wait here for ten minutes. If you haven't come back, I'll start walking to the shop. Um … you did understand what I was saying in the car?'

'About HIV being only in blood and, er … Yes, Mr Nelson. We'll get her away from them, whatever it takes.' Philomena touched a small bag that hung by her door and then stepped out into the dark.

Nelson sat and listened to her soft footsteps. He tried to be calm, but found he couldn't sit still. Philomena, a grown woman with intelligence and some education, hadn't known basic facts about HIV. How many others still misunderstood this infection?

He looked at his watch. Only two minutes gone. Philomena had some cheap but clean furniture and there was a shelf with some books on. He opened one and read a few paragraphs. He looked round the curtain into the other room and saw a bed and a wardrobe in there.

He checked his watch. Eight minutes had gone. Long enough, he decided. He switched off the light. The door made almost no noise as he opened and then closed it. He stood outside for a few moments to get used to the dark.

But before he could do anything, he heard quiet voices and footsteps coming towards him. Philomena was bringing the children to her house.

Nelson could see that Lily Anne was in a state of shock. Her breathing was irregular and her eyes wide and unblinking. Philomena was carrying Blessing. He was asleep.

Nelson and Philomena made a bed for them on the sofa. Lily Anne sat on the edge, beside the sleeping Blessing, looking at her pink shoes. Philomena made some hot milk from milk powder. Nelson sat down on a chair by the sofa and took one of Lily Anne's hands gently in his.

'Lily Anne, I know you've had a shock. But please try to tell me what happened,' Nelson said gently.

She looked up into his face, her eyes full of tears. 'It was my fault,' she said. 'It was all my fault and now they'll take the house away from us and we'll have nothing, and I have to pay for the broken vase.'

Nelson and Philomena looked at each other in surprise. Philomena made a sign and Nelson got up and went out. He stood just outside the door, listening.

Nelson heard Philomena sit on the chair by Lily Anne.

'Why is it *your* fault?' she asked.

Lily Anne took a deep breath. 'I got food from Mr Nakula without paying. Ever since Dad died, if we had no money, I knew I could get food there if I smiled at him.'

'Smiled?' Philomena asked.

'Yes. I saw the girls at the bottle store smile at the men who go there. Then the men would give them money. So I used that smile on Mr Nakula.'

'I see,' said Philomena.

'I know what it means, that smile.' Lily Anne's voice held a hint of a boast. 'I know it means, "I'll let you have sex with me one day." But I knew Mr Nakula was afraid of Mum, too. So I thought I'd never have to pay the debt …'

'So when you called and asked me how to stop it if the brothers tried something, you weren't asking "just in case". You knew they would.' Philomena sounded a bit cross.

'Yes, Aunt Philomena. I didn't tell you everything. I'm sorry. And your idea of telling them that Mum's ghost was watching me stopped them for a while. But … I think Mr Nakula's brother is sick. He smells like Dad did. I think he wanted …' Lily Anne made a sound as though she was going to be sick.

Nelson heard Philomena move quickly and then Lily Anne was noisily sick into something plastic.

'OK, now, Lily Anne. It's OK now,' whispered Philomena. 'Sick it all out. You'll be better when it's gone.'

Blessing began to stir. Philomena appeared at the door.

'Please come in now, Mr Nelson. We have to decide what to do,' she said in a low voice.

Nelson came in and sat down quietly beside Lily Anne while Philomena gave Blessing some milk in a cup. This made him cough.

Lily Anne took the cup from Philomena. 'He can eat and drink most days,' she said. 'But sometimes he's too sick.'

Philomena looked at Nelson and they went outside.

She said, 'I'm afraid to have them both here, with Blessing HIV positive, and perhaps Lily Anne too.'

Nelson was thinking. He couldn't remember how many rooms for staff there were at his home.

'And Lily Anne has told me, Mr Nelson,' Philomena went on, 'that she has started her monthly bleeding. It's difficult to keep her clean here, with no water in the house. There's an empty room at your house, in the staff cottage where we live. Could we take them there, just for tonight?'

Nelson was relieved. 'Of course, Philomena. That would be best. They can stay a day or two and we'll get them to a clinic for tests. Just try not to let my mother see them!'

# Chapter 8    *The hospice*

Nelson had to be at the hotel all the next day, but Philomena took the children for HIV tests. When Nelson got home she told him that Blessing was definitely HIV positive and that Lily Anne was negative so far. Philomena had also been out to Sector D on the bus to pay for the vase with money Nelson had given her, and get the children's things. She'd told Mrs Chivasa what had happened, but Mr and Mrs Mbizi knew nothing about it.

Nelson ate alone as neither of his parents was at home, and then went up to his room and began searching the Internet again for an organisation that could help.

Some time later, he found the name of a hospice that took in people who were dying of AIDS, so that they could die peacefully and with less pain. There was no website, but there was a phone number and it seemed to be in an area about half an hour by car from Sector D.

'At last!' he said to himself, and dialed on his mobile.

'Hello, Saint John's Hospice.' It was a woman's voice with a strong Irish accent. 'How can we help?'

'Good evening. I … I've met a family of orphans in Sector D in Chapangana who need help. They've had to move out of their home. Do you take in children?' Nelson asked.

'We try to help people with AIDS in their own homes.' The woman sounded warm and caring. 'Are they HIV positive?'

'Right … Well, they have no home now, and the youngest one is. But he's very small and his sister won't leave him.'

'And they have nowhere to go. How old is the sister?' Nelson could hear a smile in the woman's voice.

'She's twelve, I think. Could you take them both?'

'Would you like to bring them over for a look first?'

'Yes. Thanks. My name is Nelson. And you are?'

'I'm Sister Michael.'

'Sister Michael? Right. Thank you, Sister Michael. May I bring them tomorrow morning, before I go to work?'

'You may. See you then, young man.'

Nelson put the phone down with a smile on his face. If this went well, the children would be gone and safe before his parents knew anything about them. He went down to the kitchen to get a drink before he slept. As he passed his parents' bedroom door he heard drawers opening and shutting and feet moving around. He knocked. His mother came to the door, closing it behind her.

'Are you OK, Mum?' he asked. 'You sound very busy for the middle of the night.'

'Yes. I'm fine. Just sorting out some clothes for next week. I have a lot of things to do in the next few days.' Ruby looked very tired and had taken off her make-up.

'Can I help you?' Nelson asked.

Ruby laughed. 'Of course not! What do you know about what I need to wear? Go to bed and get some sleep.'

\* \* \*

At the hospice early next morning, Sister Michael showed Nelson and Lily Anne round the whole place. Sister Michael was white and in her sixties, with the most caring blue eyes Nelson had ever seen. There were three long low buildings in the shade of a group of tall, dusty flamboyant trees. Each building had rooms with one or two beds in. Most of the patients were adults. There were just a few rooms for children. Each patient had a bed, two meals and a wash each day, and someone to take care of them. Everyone worked voluntarily and nobody had to pay. What money the hospice had, came from the church and as gifts.

A very thin man was making an old door into a bed for Blessing as they looked around. When they'd finished, Lily Anne took Blessing to the bookshelves and started to read a book to him. Other children gathered round to listen.

Once he saw the children could stay and were settled, Nelson gave some money to Sister Michael.

'Sure, you don't have to do that, you know,' she said.

'But it will help, won't it?' Nelson said with a smile.

'Well, I won't say no. You're a very kind young man.'

Nelson drove home, through miles of suburbs that looked like Sector D. 'How many more orphans are there out there,' he thought, 'and how few places like the hospice? So little hope …'

'And when,' he asked himself later, as he drove up to his house, 'when am I going to have the courage to call Viki and ask her to come and make another programme about them?'

* * *

Later, in the free moments during his working day, Nelson thought about what to say to Viki. He wanted a good reason for calling her: at least better than 'I can't get you out of my mind although I know you couldn't care less, so please can we meet up?' Finally, his work finished, and with a yellow moon rising in front of him, he drove over to see Daniel.

Daniel looked very tired. He'd got a part-time job working as a singing advertisement, outside a music shop in the centre of town. He went there three afternoons a week and stood outside the shop with a sign saying, 'Every song you've ever heard is on sale here!' His job was also to sing a few lines from some of the most popular songs to persuade passers-by to come in and spend their money. For this he was paid a tiny amount. But at least he could give Mrs Chivasa something towards his keep, although he had to do most of his school work on Sundays.

Daniel told Nelson about this as they sat in Mrs Chivasa's tiny garden on her blue chairs, in the light of the lamp over her front door.

Nelson told Daniel about Saint John's Hospice.

'I have to thank you again and again, Nelson,' Daniel said. 'Now we'll be OK for a while. That's just incredible.' After a moment, he added, 'Do you know how long they'll let Lily Anne stay at the hospice?'

'Probably until little Blessing ...' Nelson sighed. 'You know he's going to die, don't you?'

Daniel looked at his long thin feet and nodded his head.

'Then Lily Anne's going to be homeless again,' said Nelson. 'So I've been thinking how you can earn some more money, and maybe you can all move back home.'

'And how is that?' asked Daniel without enthusiasm.

'I thought,' said Nelson, 'if those TV people came back, and filmed you doing a real performance, then maybe people would pay you to come and sing at parties and ...'

'Will they come back?' Daniel's eyes lit up.

'Well, I could phone Phil, or the reporter woman ...'

Daniel jumped up and started a gentle dance. He spoke to the rhythm of his dance. *'You've seen me on TV, now you see the real me. Nelson, that's so cool, better than the biggest jewel, better than a day off school!'*

People passing in the road joined in and soon there were thirty people dancing and laughing in the moonlight.

\* \* \*

When Nelson got home, he could hear his mother talking on the phone in the sitting room. Her voice was quiet but angry. He would have pitied the person on the other end, except that he guessed it was his father. He went upstairs to his room, where he took a deep breath and dialled Viki's number on his mobile. He got, 'This phone is switched off. Please try later.' He sent a text message: 'News from Sector D. Pls call.'

He still felt like two people, one completely in love with Viki, and the other embarrassed at his own stupidity. 'It was better she had her phone switched off,' he thought.

When his phone rang later, he was on the Internet.

'Hello?' His voice didn't seem like his own.

'Who am I speaking to?' Viki was bored and tired, but her voice still made his legs go weak.

'My name's Nelson Mbizi. I ... Well, I know Daniel Mawadza, the boy who sings.'

'Yeah. So what's the news?'

'He's made some new songs and he's now singing at the 7th Street Shopping Mall in the afternoons, but the family has had to split up. I felt you might want to do a new piece on him.'

'Has he had an offer from a record company?'

'Not yet, but I thought another piece on your programme might make him a bit more well-known and ...'

53

'Look, I work for the news department of a TV station. We're not in the business of getting every parentless kid in Africa started with his music career. Get me some real news, and until you do, keep off my phone!'

'Just a minute!' Nelson suddenly had an idea. 'Daniel was afraid his sister was paying for food with sex. He just wants to give her a better chance.'

'Say that again.' Viki's energy had returned.

'When the family had to rent their house out so they wouldn't starve, Daniel's sister went to live with a family that wanted her to pay with sex.'

'Where is she now?'

'At a church hospice.'

'So she's safe?' Viki sounded almost disappointed.

'Yes, for now, but they can't keep her forever. It's an AIDS hospice and she's HIV negative – so far.'

'The family that had her, they still around?'

'Yes.' Nelson smiled to himself. Viki *was* interested.

'Can you meet me at nine o'clock tomorrow morning at the Lion Hills Hotel?'

Nelson's mouth suddenly went dry. 'Why there?'

'Because I'm staying there,' Viki said impatiently. 'I just got off a plane. Why do you think my phone was off?'

'I ... I work at that hotel,' Nelson stammered.

'Right. So it's no problem to meet in the morning?'

'No. Of course not.' Nelson could hardly breathe.

'You going to tell me how I'll know you?' she asked.

'Er ... I'll know you. My name's ...'

'Nelson Mbizi, wasn't it? Yeah, I remember. See you in reception, nine o'clock.'

'Bye,' he said, but she'd already hung up.

# Chapter 9  *Turning point*

It was hard to concentrate on anything after that, so Nelson went downstairs to watch TV. He was just getting sleepy when his mother came into the room.

'Could you come through and talk to your father, Nelson?' she said.

'It's midnight, Mum. Is anything wrong?'

'Just come. Please.' She had an expression on her face he'd never seen before. As he followed her into the main sitting room he realised it was controlled panic.

His parents stood in silence on either side of a small table. On it, there were a lot of papers in tidy heaps.

'What's wrong?' Nelson asked as he went in. His father looked up from the papers. He looked ten years older and two sizes smaller.

'I've been getting threatening phone calls for weeks,' said Mr Mbizi, his eyes showing white, his voice thin with fear. 'But today a friend warned me that someone is trying to get rid of me completely.'

'They say he's stolen a lot of money,' added Ruby.

Nelson stared. He'd guessed there was something wrong, of course, but he'd expected it to be more personal. This, he knew, could mean life or death.

'I've made arrangements to leave the country for a short time,' his father said. 'I hope it won't be necessary to stay away for long, but it may be. Your mother doesn't want to come with me.'

Nelson breathed in. He couldn't believe what he was hearing. 'What ... do you want me to do?'

'The problems are with the government. Business is fine. So I want you to stand in for me until I can get back.'

'What! Are you sure?' Nelson stared at his father. 'I thought you thought I'm not ready.'

'Well, you've shown me lately that you do have a bit of initiative. And anyway, you'll be more loyal than the managers, who might steal everything the minute my back is turned.'

'Oh, right,' said Nelson in surprise.

'We've all these papers to sign,' Mr Mbizi growled.

'The lawyer's on her way – Mrs Murape,' said Ruby.

Nelson looked at her. 'You staying then, Mum?'

'I'm waiting for the lawyer to tell me. If she says it's OK, I will. If not, I'll go to my cousin's in London.'

Nelson sat down at the table with his father. His mind was fighting its way out of the fog of shock. 'When are you leaving?' he asked.

'In about an hour,' his father answered.

'An hour!' Nelson shook his head to clear it and then sat with his father making lists of things he would need to do. It reminded him of the checklists he'd learned when he was studying, and that helped him to concentrate.

Mrs Murape arrived and explained to Nelson and Ruby what each was responsible for. They signed all the papers. Mrs Murape thought it was best for Ruby to leave as well. According to the law, as his wife, Ruby could be held responsible for any money Mr Mbizi supposedly owed, whereas his son could not.

Washington assured his son that he hadn't taken any money. 'There's a large sum missing from government funds – billions – and I have enemies of course. So they can kill two birds with one stone if they accuse me of taking it. The real thief gets away with it, they kill the import-export bill, and I'm out of the way in prison – or dead and shamed.' Nelson shook his head in silent disbelief.

Then it was time to go, so Nelson helped Ruby and Washington down with their two small suitcases. He shook his father's hand and then hugged his mother for a long time. She whispered in his ear, 'We may not be back at all, so it's all yours now. Take care of it.' Far too soon he found himself standing at the front door, waving goodbye to his parents, wondering when he would see them again. His father had said to him, 'Don't let anyone know that I've left the country. Just say you don't know where I am. Say we had a fight. Everyone will believe that!' Nobody had smiled.

As the white gate closed behind the Mercedes, Nelson turned back into the house and locked the door.

He had never felt so alone. He was now responsible for hundreds of workers, one large and two smaller hotels, a traditional farm in the village that his father came from and this house. And he had no idea how long this would be for.

At least he knew now what all the 'only legal son' business had been about. He was grateful to his mother for protecting his right to take over from his father, but it had all happened so quickly that he didn't know where to start.

He took all the papers and account books up to his bedroom and began looking through them.

\* \* \*

At five o'clock the phone in the hall rang. Nelson went down to answer it. It was the gate. There were four policemen in a truck who wanted to speak to his father. Mrs Murape had warned him this might happen.

He ran up and hid the books and papers in his old toy box and took off his clothes. He was in his nightclothes when he unlocked the front door. Two of the policemen stood there with a large dog. They had guns.

'Mr Washington Mbizi?' the taller one said.

'He isn't here at the moment,' Nelson answered, trying to look as if he'd just woken up.

'Where is he?'

'I'm not sure. He doesn't usually tell me where he's going.'

'When will he be back?'

'I don't know … Why do you want him?'

'He's been stealing money from the government. We have to search the house.'

'What? Is that allowed? Don't you have to have …?' Nelson made a gesture to stop them.

'Just stand aside. We need to know if he's here.'

They pushed through the door. One of the other men came in and stood beside Nelson in the hallway. The first two and the dog checked all the rooms. There were no signs of the Mbizis' packing. Ruby had been careful. The tall policeman made a phone call asking for all airports and borders to be watched. As he was leaving, he turned to Nelson and said, 'Don't leave town. We'll need to talk to you again very soon.'

# Chapter 10  *Viki gets to work*

When they'd gone, Nelson couldn't rest. Had his parents got away? Were they still on the road? He tried to call his mother's mobile. It was out of range.

He got out the papers and copied everything he could onto his laptop computer. He thought he might be followed, so he put the originals in his tennis bag and the laptop in a shopping bag. He knew he'd have to keep that with him from now on. He borrowed the truck again and left for the hotel at his usual time. The tennis bag was on the floor beside him. Nobody stopped him on the road. When he got to the hotel, he locked the tennis bag up in the hotel strongroom.

Fletcher didn't seem surprised that Nelson was now his boss. He said Mr Mbizi had warned him it might be necessary for a while. Fletcher's calmness steadied Nelson's nerves as they worked on the accounts together.

At eight fifty-five, his heartbeat shaking his whole body, Nelson said, 'Excuse me, Fletcher. I have an appointment at nine. We'll go on with this later.'

Viki was standing at reception as Nelson came out of the lift. She was wearing jeans and a dark green top.

'Good morning. I'm Nelson Mbizi,' he managed to say.

'Hi,' she said, looking him up and down. 'I want you to tell me all about Daniel's sister …' The fire in her eyes held a threat, even though she was small and only came up to his chest.

'Let's have some breakfast,' Nelson said. He felt faint. One half of him felt sick with wanting to put his arms around her, the other felt angry at himself – and very tired.

They ate in the restaurant on the roof. Viki asked about Lily Anne and wrote notes. She wanted to know where Lily Anne was, but Nelson felt he should talk to Sister Michael before he told her. Viki was almost friendly, until she suddenly asked, 'You ill or something?'

Nelson sighed. 'No, not ill. I've been working all night.'

'Well, I hope they pay you properly for that.' Viki took a mouthful of her breakfast and chewed it slowly.

Nelson watched her. 'When do you go back to Jo'burg?'

'I should manage to do this new story and the one I came for in two days.' She took another mouthful.

'Would you like to meet me for a meal tonight, when you finish work?'

'Maybe …' She licked her lips. 'Can you take me to the Black Umbrella? I heard it's the best place in town.'

The Black Umbrella was very expensive. But suddenly Nelson remembered he was boss of a new world, *and* he was making a date with Viki.

'I'll see what I can do,' he said, pleased with himself.

'If you can afford that,' she said, her eyes wide and innocent, 'you could afford to help those orphans.'

Nelson just stared at her. He didn't even feel angry. She smiled a poisonous little smile and drank some coffee.

'Come to think of it,' he said quietly after a moment's thought, 'you're right. I've just been … promoted. So soon I should be able to help more.'

'Why? Don't you have enough money now?'

Nelson suddenly remembered that she was a reporter and that his father's disappearance would be big news for her. He decided not to mention his father at all.

'Not of my own,' Nelson said, looking down at his plate.

'So this promotion means you will have?' asked Viki.

'Yes. Now I'm taking over much more of the management of the hotels. I studied that in the UK, you see.'

'Right.' Viki drank some coffee. 'And how many of your employees are HIV positive, do you think?'

Nelson was glad to change the subject away from the danger of mentioning his father. 'That's something I need to learn more about,' he said.

'Yeah. Exactly.' Viki's voice had an aggressive edge. 'You realise you could lose about a quarter of your workers in the next ten years? You need to be training extra people to take their places, putting money in the bank to help their families.'

'People don't like to talk about ...' Nelson interrupted.

'Very few companies realise the extent of the problem.' Viki tore open a bread roll and began buttering one half.

'True,' Nelson said. 'It's something I shall certainly be researching into.' He thought, 'This isn't what I want to talk about, however right she is.'

'Research doesn't help.' Viki was dismissive. 'Telling people helps. Making it public helps. When it's in the papers, businesses have to take notice.'

Nelson felt exhausted. He paused while she finished her coffee, then said, 'Would you like some more?'

'No, that's enough. I'm meeting Phil in five minutes.'

'So shall I pick you up around nine tonight?' he asked.

'I usually eat earlier. Can you make it seven?'

'Sure. I'll call your room at seven.'

She didn't speak as she turned away, just lifted a hand.

Nelson stood up politely. 'Why do I want her?' he asked himself, feeling sick and stupid. 'I must be mad.'

He arranged to see all the department managers in the afternoon and then went home. It must seem as much as possible like an ordinary day, so he told Philomena and Cook he was taking his midday break early. They didn't ask about his parents and he didn't mention them. He was too tired to think up explanations. Anyway, the man at the gate would have been gossiping about the cars in the night and the police at dawn. Nelson sat down to look through the documents on his computer, but his head sank onto the desk and he slept.

*   *   *

Daniel had a visit from Viki and Phil that afternoon at the Chivasas' house. They asked him about Lily Anne and the Nakulas and where they lived, and they left to interview them without asking Daniel to join them. He wondered what Viki was going to do, so he ran along the footpaths between the houses and arrived at the shop just as they drove up. He watched Viki and Phil get out of their truck and walk to the shop door. He stood half-hidden by a fence and saw Tobias come out with another man. Viki moved the two men into the sun, and Phil began shooting with the camera on his shoulder.

Daniel heard Viki say, 'That was a very good thing you did – taking in orphan children – that was very kind.' Was her smile a little sexy? Her eyes were wide and clear green. A small crowd gathered to watch. Daniel joined it.

Tobias looked very pleased. 'Melanie Mawadza was a good customer,' he said with an oily smile.

'And this gentleman is …?' Viki asked.

'This is Arthur, my brother. He has lived with us since his wife died.' Tobias went on smiling, looking at the camera. Daniel had never seen Arthur before, only heard of him.

'So you are both single?' Viki was being warm and friendly. Daniel didn't recognise her as the same woman.

'That's right.' Tobias turned his attention to Viki.

'And there are no other women in your house except your mother?'

'That's right. Mum looks after us well.'

Viki turned to Arthur with a sweet look in her eyes. 'Is Lily Anne a good child? Did she behave herself properly in your home?' Arthur's eyes were red, his skin dry and dull.

'Well,' began Arthur with a frown.

But Tobias touched his arm and he smiled. 'Yeah,' he said. 'But in the end, she was only here for a day.'

Viki laughed a playful little laugh. 'A day and a night, wasn't it?' Daniel moved closer.

'Mmm,' Arthur went on smiling stiffly.

'Did she give you money for her food?'

'Nah. We didn't want her money,' said Arthur. He licked his bleeding lips slowly. 'She just helped Mum. We were happy to feed her and her brother for that.'

Viki laughed sexily again, her voice soft and caring. 'So there was nothing else in your agreement with her?'

'She's a bit young to do anything else for us.' Tobias laughed. Then he whispered, 'Not experienced, like you.'

'I thought twelve-year-olds were very attractive to older men? Making love to young ones can stop AIDS, can't it?'

Viki's eyes were dancing with friendly laughter.

Tobias nodded his head and said, 'Yes, well, we talked about it, but we decided against it.'

'Did you talk to *her* about it?' Viki leaned towards them again, her voice quiet and knowing.

'Nah,' said Tobias, almost touching Viki as his long tongue licked his lips. 'We let her sleep.'

Viki's voice changed to icy cold, although she didn't move. 'You had some trouble with a vase, didn't you?'

Tobias frowned in confusion and looked at Arthur, then Viki. 'What? What do you mean?'

'Oh, you know very well what I mean.' Viki stood back and looked a question at Phil. He nodded. She turned back to the Nakula family. 'Nothing will stop AIDS if you've got it, Mr Nakula. Not medicine from the medicine man, not sex with little girls, not eating special plants. You should get your brother to hospital today!'

She turned and walked fast to the TV truck. Phil followed. Tobias started to shout after her, but Daniel didn't wait to hear, and ran back to the Chivasas' house.

And there, after some very polite chat with Mrs Chivasa, Viki told Daniel he could sing again.

'What are you going to say about me?' Daniel asked Viki.

'I'll say that sometimes you find work now, singing in public, so that you can help pay for your sister to be in a safe place. Then you can sing any song you like,' Viki said.

'Can you say I'm always looking for more work?'

'No, Daniel. This isn't an advertisement for you. It's a piece of news about what happens to some families when both parents die: the dangers, and how kids manage.'

'Right. So a song about my mum would be OK?'

'If you want. Or a love song might be a better one – get you more work …' She looked up at him, eyebrow raised.

'You're not so bad, Miss Viki,' Daniel said.

'Shut up and get on with it,' said Viki, almost smiling.

So Daniel sat down under Mrs Chivasa's lemon tree. Phil turned the camera on him and Daniel said, 'This is a love song to my mother. She died eighteen days ago.'

He played a gentle tune and sang:

*Love's a light, sun through dust.*
*Keeps shining through with hope and trust.*
*You're flying now and we're past the worst.*
*Your body's gone, dust to dust.*
*But don't fly too far, at least, not yet.*
*Stay nearby until I get*
*A new cell phone to dial the sky,*
*So we can talk instead of cry.*

By the time he finished a small crowd had appeared and they clapped as the last notes of the mbira died away.

Phil turned the camera onto them and then to Viki, who said, 'Daniel can make you laugh and cry at the same time. He sings to make money to pay for his sister to live in a safe place and to buy traditional medicine for his little brother, who is HIV positive. The family have rented out their house to pay for food and Daniel's school fees and music lessons. One day he wants to make records.

'Daniel and his family are the lucky ones. They have a house and perhaps a future. But most orphans in Sector D, and all the other places like it, have no hope. They die because they're sick or because they can't earn enough money to pay for food. Some grandmothers are caring for more than ten children. Some children become thieves or sell their bodies so they can eat. They don't know where to get help. The medicines used in America and Europe to fight AIDS are unavailable or too expensive.

'Each one of you watching this programme must think about these children. AIDS is here to stay and will kill between a quarter and a third of your family, friends and colleagues here in Africa in the next ten years. We all need to learn about it; how to live our lives and help others live theirs as happily as possible with this killer beside us.

'Thank you, Daniel, for your song, and thank you, Mrs Chivasa, for giving Daniel a happy home and the chance of a future.' Phil nodded to Viki and turned off the camera.

They shook Mrs Chivasa's hand and Viki walked off.

Daniel asked Phil, 'Did you come because Nelson called you?'

'Yeah. He got in touch with me, then Viki. They had breakfast together this morning. Why?' Phil's eyes went to the car where Viki was now in the driver's seat, waiting.

'He got my sister and brother away from the Nakulas. It'd be good if you put something about him in the film.'

'Viki may be going to. She's having dinner with him tonight. I'll suggest it if I get the chance.'

'Great. Thanks. And thanks for having me sing on TV – twice! Today was better ... the first time was too soon.'

Phil walked to the truck. 'Yeah. Keep my number!'

'Thanks. Bye.' Daniel watched them drive off. It looked as though Viki was angry with Phil again.

# Chapter 11 *First date*

Nelson was excited and nervous that evening. After his morning sleep, his mind was clearer. He'd had meetings with each of the department managers to tell them about the new arrangements and hear their comments. He'd asked his father's secretary to book him a table for two at a very nice restaurant on the edge of town with tables in the garden, fish ponds, and lamps in the trees. (After Viki's comment, he'd decided against the Black Umbrella.) He'd spent some more time looking at HIV charity websites. He had the beginnings of an idea about how to help the situation in Sector D, so he sent off some emails for information.

He'd also called home trying to sound normal. Cook said she hadn't seen his father, but that he'd phoned. The message was that they'd arrived fine in the village and they'd be back in a day or two. Nelson knew that meant they were safely across the border.

He'd relaxed a little then, but now he was tense again as he called Viki's room.

'Hi, Nelson? Five minutes?' she said, and hung up.

He noticed his mobile battery had run out, so he left it charging with his laptop in his office, locked the door and went to get the truck. He waited for Viki at the hotel door. She came down the steps looking perfect in a smart brown trouser suit and crisp white blouse. Nelson's legs went weak again. 'I'm glad I'm sitting down,' he thought.

'Did you get to Sector D?' he asked as they drove off.

'I met the Nakulas and got them on film admitting they'd been thinking about having sex with Lily Anne.'

'My God!' Nelson exclaimed. 'How did you manage that? And what will you do with it?'

'Nothing. I'll just show it on air. It may help other girls to protect themselves, though most people in Sector D won't see it. It's a good thing they didn't manage to rape her. The brother, Arthur, is really sick. He'll be dead in a year.'

'How can you be sure?'

'He's as skinny as spaghetti. His lips are bleeding and he's burning up with fever.' Viki sounded disgusted.

After a moment, Nelson asked, 'Did Daniel sing again?'

'Yeah. He sang a song about his mother.'

Her voice changed. Nelson glanced across at her. 'What's wrong, Viki? Wasn't he good?'

'Yeah, yeah. Of course he was good. It was a very sad song, that's all.' She was businesslike again.

'Have you ...' Nelson hesitated. 'Have you lost your mother too?'

'No, no.' Viki laughed a tired little laugh. 'My mum's still fine, looking after my brothers and sisters in Soweto.'

'So ...?' Nelson dared to ask.

'So nothing ...' She was silent for a minute. 'Is it your job to decide on the colours in the rooms of the hotel, because mine's a really sick purple?'

'No. I only started a couple of weeks ago.'

'So what *do* you do?'

Nelson told her about his job as boss of three hotels. He was afraid she'd ask about his father, but she didn't.

At the restaurant, Viki asked to sit near the largest fish pond. She wanted to be able to watch the fish swimming in the dark water. The waiter moved their table to a place on the grass, and then lit a little lamp on it for them.

'Why did you ask me to dinner?' Viki asked as soon as they were alone.

He smiled to hide his surprise, and said, 'Because you're beautiful ...'

Viki had a 'You must be joking' expression on her face.

'... but you seem ... troubled. And,' he went on, 'you may not know many people here, so I thought you might be alone tonight.'

Viki laughed out loud. 'Well, at least you said what you thought straight out,' she said.

'You're very straight with everyone yourself.'

'Yeah ...' Viki looked at the pond.

There was a little pause. A small waterfall played into the pond and large, lazy goldfish caught the light. A waiter came to take their order.

'What's your other story on this trip?' Nelson asked when he'd gone.

'It's about a chocolate factory.'

'Chocolate!' he exclaimed. He thought, 'At least it's not disappearing members of the government.'

'Yes.' She was gazing at the shining fish.

She didn't explain, so Nelson said, 'Chocolate and children orphaned by AIDS. Is your work always so varied?'

'Mmm ... The AIDS message is the most important.'

'Yes. AIDS has changed everyone's lives.'

Viki looked at him sharply. 'Has it changed yours?'

'Only to make me careful! But for other people it's ...'

'A life or death business.' Viki's voice was hard. She was looking at the tablecloth.

'Have *you* lost someone lately?' Nelson asked gently.

'Not yet. But it's only a matter of time.' Viki looked up at him again.

'Do you want to talk about it?'

'Not really ... What I do want is to make as much noise as I can. It's good I have a job where I can make some things more well-known. So that's what I do. I tell the world about AIDS as it is, not all the stories and lies.'

'I've been thinking,' Nelson said, 'about what you said – about those kids and a better place to live.'

'Yeah. You're a rich man. You could do a lot for them.'

'Yes, maybe I could. I haven't got much spare time just now, but I'm beginning to think that those people in Sector D need a place to go, a kind of ... a kind of AIDS centre.'

'What would they do there?' Viki spoke sharply.

'Talk about it, learn about it, get tested ...'

'Ha! They'd never even go in the door.' Viki seemed suddenly angrier than ever. 'Nobody wants to know about AIDS. They just want to pretend it doesn't exist. People who are dying now, this minute, bleeding and coughing to death, even they don't want to know what they've got.'

'Perhaps ...' Nelson decided not to argue.

The waiter brought their food.

'What you really need,' Viki said a few moments later, 'is a programme in schools to tell the kids the truth. And a government programme that tests everyone for free and gives advice. Then everyone who's HIV positive should get those drugs that slow it down – anti-retrovirals – for free as well.'

'Yes, I know. ARVs. But can you imagine any government in Africa doing that? Any government in the world, even?'

'That's what it needs, though. And in some places they are doing at least some of those things.'

'But what about people who have AIDS now?' Nelson thought of little Blessing. 'They need state help too. You've got to care for the dying and orphans as well.'

'The sick are sick. They aren't going to get better. Just give them ARVs and let them die when their time comes. But to stop HIV spreading we *must* spend the money on making sure they don't infect anyone else.'

'How can you say that?' Nelson was horrified. 'Even some animals take care of their dying relatives.'

'Not if they have to choose between the dying and the living. And that's what we humans have to do now. There just isn't enough money to care for those who have no future *and* to make sure everyone else *has* a future.'

Nelson was silent. Viki was getting more angry by the minute, and he didn't want to have a real fight with her.

'People who test positive these days have to learn to look after themselves,' she went on. There was a pause.

'Shall we try talking about something else?' he asked.

'Sorry?'

'You were the one who said I was rich enough to help Daniel's family. And when I talk about doing just that, you get really angry, as though I was wrong. So I thought we should talk about something that doesn't make you angry.'

'I didn't say you're wrong to help *them*. Except for Blessing, they're still OK. They do have a future. But it's not enough just to give them food and get them back home.

They need telling again and again how to avoid getting sick. Nobody does that.'

'Except you, you mean?' Nelson smiled. 'Nobody else in this whole world is trying to get that message across.'

Viki looked at him as if he were five years old. 'There *are* others. But not enough, and not in the right places.'

'Right. OK ...' Perhaps she was like his mother, and couldn't accept other people's opinions. He smiled again and said, 'Now we *are* going to talk about something else.'

'Like what?' Her voice gave him no encouragement.

'Like why you agreed to come out to dinner with me.'

Viki looked up from her plate. It was as if she was seeing him for the first time. 'God knows!' she said.

Nelson felt a real pain in his chest. 'Well ... thanks.'

'You're welcome.'

He thought, 'So ... This really isn't going to work. She doesn't like me at all.' He ate some more of his suddenly tasteless food. 'Maybe she just thinks I'm useful to her in some way. But then at least she would be polite ... So what *is* wrong between us?' He was quiet a long time, trying to accept the pain and forget that his body wanted hers.

At last he said, 'There is one thing I want to ask you.'

Viki was finishing the last of her food with a slight frown. 'Mmm?'

'Are there any centres in Soweto for people with HIV and AIDS – like I mentioned? Somewhere to go and learn what to do and meet other people with the same problems?'

'Not in my area. I think I've heard of one further away. But people are embarrassed to be seen going there.' Viki sighed. 'That's so stupid, but it's the way things are.'

'So you don't advise me to do anything like that?'

'Why should I advise you to do anything?'

'Well, you know more people with AIDS than I do.'

'What do you mean?' She was angry again. 'I've just met the people I make reports about.'

'Well, that's more than I have.'

Viki looked at her watch. 'Look. Can we leave soon?'

'Yes, I … Of course.'

'I'll just go to the toilet.'

'Sure …' Nelson stood up as Viki left the table. He sat down again and watched the lights on the water.

When she got back, he'd paid the bill and they left immediately. Viki was silent. Nelson was trying to think. She obviously wasn't interested in him, not for himself or even for his money. It was as if she'd locked a door against him.

Getting out of the truck, she said, 'It was a good meal.'

His voice had an edge. 'Thanks for eating it with me.'

'No problem.'

'Tell me something, Viki.'

She stopped on the steps and turned round. 'Yeah?'

'Why does a beautiful, intelligent girl like you enjoy hating so much?'

Viki's mouth and eyes opened in surprise. She turned and ran up the steps without answering.

Nelson sat in the truck for a few moments. The angry, painful fog in his head suddenly cleared. 'Right,' he thought. 'That's over. Finished. Forget her.' He got out of the truck, threw the keys to the doorman and started up the steps himself.

Suddenly he felt his arms being held from behind and a voice in his ear said, 'Come with us, please, Mr Mbizi. You're under arrest.'

# Chapter 12   *Where's your father?*

Nelson was dragged into a waiting van and found himself lying in complete darkness on the metal floor. He rolled from side to side as the van raced along. His head hit against something and he lost consciousness.

When he came round, he was on a hard bed in a cell. There was a bucket in the corner as a toilet. There was another man asleep and snoring on the other bed. The place was disgusting and smelled of dirt and alcohol.

A man with keys came and took Nelson to a room with two chairs with a desk between.

'Sit there and don't move, otherwise we'll have to tie you up,' said the man. He went out and locked the door.

Nelson's head was aching, but his mind was working. This must be to do with his father. His heart beat with fear as he heard the key in the door.

A tall man wearing a black leather jacket came in and sat down opposite Nelson.

'Nelson Mbizi,' said the man, and just looked at Nelson.

Nelson acted stupid. 'Yes?' he said pleasantly.

'Where's your father?' asked the man. He had a pair of sunglasses and was polishing them on his black shirt. The sunglasses showed he wasn't an ordinary policeman. He was from the secret police of the Intelligence Agency.

'I had a message that he was in the village, so he'll probably be back in a day or two.' Nelson tried to relax, although his head ached and his heart was racing.

'He's not in the village,' said the man.

Nelson looked surprised. 'Then I don't know where he is,' he said worriedly.

'Where's your father?' the man said again.

'If he's not in the village, I don't know,' Nelson said.

'Where's your father?' the man said a third time.

'Look, I don't know. I thought he was in the village.' Nelson was glad he really didn't know where his father was.

The man stood up and put on a pair of black leather gloves. 'You know,' he stated.

Nelson stood up too, expecting to be hit. 'I really don't know. I've been out of the country for three years. I got back less than three weeks ago. I have no idea what you're trying to find out or why you want my father.'

The man stared into Nelson's face for what felt like an hour. Then he turned and left the room, banging the door.

Nelson sat down, feeling quite sick.

The door opened again. A different man took Nelson by the arm and led him back towards the cell.

Nelson said, 'Look, you … you can't hold me here. I haven't done anything wrong. I want to speak to my lawyer.'

'In the morning,' this man said, and pushed Nelson back into the cell and locked the door.

Nelson lost his temper. He shook the door, but nothing happened. He walked up and down shouting. The other man slept on. In the end, Nelson sat on the bed, exhausted. 'The worst day of my life,' he thought. 'If I get out of this alive, I'll never have anything to do with politics. I'll get that AIDS centre started – and I'll forget all about Viki.'

\* \* \*

Nelson had eventually dropped off to sleep and woke curled up on the hard bed. Two policemen were taking the other man out of the cell. He had to be held up, he was still so drunk. Nelson followed them out.

'No, you stay in there,' said one of the policemen, trying to push him back while keeping the other man up.

'I want to see my lawyer,' said Nelson.

It seemed that the man with the sunglasses hadn't left any orders about what to do with Nelson. So Nelson signed a piece of paper and walked out into the early sunshine, trying not to show how relieved he was.

He took a taxi to the hotel. He told Fletcher what had happened and arranged to be off for the rest of the day. He collected his mobile and laptop and went home.

Philomena and Cook were very excited. A group of men from the Intelligence Agency had been there from early morning until a few minutes before. Cook guessed they'd been setting up microphones, bugging the house.

Nelson was too tired to do anything about that, or to tell them much about his arrest. 'They seem to be concerned about Mum and Dad being away. We'll just have to remember the bugs when we talk to each other – and on the phone!' he said. He went up to bed and slept.

He woke in the early afternoon and checked his emails. There was a very positive response from one large international charity. It said there could be funding of several thousand dollars if he prepared a business plan and had it approved by a bank and a lawyer. There was even an example business plan for him to work from.

He ran downstairs to find some food. Suddenly things didn't seem so bad – and he was starving!

As he was finishing his food, the afternoon newspaper came. The story about his father supposedly stealing government funds and making a run for it was all over the front page, including his own arrest. The paper did at least suggest that Mr Mbizi was being victimised. It said that the new import-export laws he'd been working on would have meant some people would lose a lot of money.

Nelson left the paper for Philomena and Cook and the gardener to read, and drove to Sector D.

*   *   *

Primrose Chivasa was tidying up after feeding Daniel, Givemore and nine other hungry, noisy children, when she heard Nelson's truck and then his 'Knock, knock!'

Silence fell. 'Come in, Mr Nelson,' she called.

After greeting everyone, Nelson asked Primrose, 'Do you know of anywhere for rent that would be big enough for a sort of club or restaurant?'

'Goodness … that's a strange question, Mr Nelson.'

Nelson laughed. 'Yes, I know – and please just call me Nelson. I want to see what the costs would be for an idea I've had.' Twelve pairs of eyes demanded an explanation. Nelson laughed again. 'Well, I hope to be able to start what they call a drop-in centre for young people in Sector D. It would have a café and music so you could meet your friends. But it would also have an office where you could get advice on living in a community with HIV and, I hope, a small laboratory where you could be tested.'

There was silence. This wasn't something people talked much about in public, in front of children. People were too afraid of HIV and AIDS. They felt helpless and hopeless, so it was spoken of behind hands, in whispers.

Nelson looked round the room. 'What do you think?'

Givemore asked, 'Would there be somewhere for a basketball ring?' and everyone laughed.

'We could make sure there was,' replied Nelson.

Daniel said quietly, 'If it was a place that people went to anyway to have fun, just a kind of social club, I think people would go, even with the laboratory. We don't have a place like that near here. But it would have to be cheap!'

Nelson looked at Mrs Chivasa. 'People would be embarrassed about the testing and advice centre?'

'Yes,' she said with emphasis.

'Right,' said Nelson. 'So is there anywhere in Sector D we could rent to be a social club with coffee and music …'

'And room to dance,' laughed Daniel.

'And for football,' shouted a smaller boy.

A man's deep voice from the door said quietly, 'I know of somewhere.' Everyone turned. It was Mr Chivasa, home from work, with a newspaper under his arm.

'I see you've been having adventures, young man,' he said to Nelson as he came in and put the paper on a shelf. Nelson touched the bruise on his head and smiled. The two men shook hands. 'Well,' went on Mr Chivasa, 'when I've eaten, I'll show you the place I've seen. It's an old bus garage by the river.'

Primrose Chivasa was disgusted. 'But that's a horrible place. It's much too dirty, and the river sometimes comes right up to it in the rains.'

'But it would be cheap,' laughed Mr Chivasa.

When Nelson, Givemore, Daniel and Mr Chivasa got to the old garage a short time later, they saw that Primrose had been right about it being dirty. But it had a large yard shaded by a great flamboyant tree just coming into leaf, and the river wasn't as close as she'd remembered.

'With a lot of work and a little money, this could be a really good place,' Nelson said after they'd looked around.

'The roof seems fine and the walls are strong,' Mr Chivasa agreed.

'Yeah!' shouted Givemore. 'You could have the basketball ring there, and the tables inside, and out here…'

'Sure,' agreed Nelson. 'And in the back part of the building, with a door from the other side, people could come to see the nurse, be tested, get advice, and so on.'

They stood outside, looking at the thin line of water running in the sandy riverbed. The river was full of rubbish and there were paths over the sand where people crossed it. When the rains came the paths and the rubbish would all be washed away.

Givemore ran down into the riverbed to get a football he could see among the rubbish. Mr Chivasa followed him. Daniel turned to Nelson.

'Did you and Miss Viki have a good time last night?'

'What do you know about that, Daniel?' Nelson asked.

'Phil said you'd be meeting up.'

'Well, we did meet. But we didn't become friends. She really seems to enjoy hurting people.'

'That's sad,' said Daniel. 'You can't stay in love with someone like that.'

Nelson laughed falsely. 'What makes you say that?'

'It's obvious. Love shines, you know, but …'

'Well, if I was in love with her before, I'm not now!'

Daniel looked at Nelson. 'No. Of course not,' he said.

Givemore and his father were coming back up from the

riverbed with the football. 'It's got a hole in it. But Dad says he can fix it!' Givemore shouted.

'Some things can't be mended,' Nelson called back.

'It depends on what you want them to do,' said Daniel.

As they walked back, Nelson asked Mr Chivasa, 'If people knew there was some help available, if they knew there was some hope, would they feel better about being seen going for blood tests?'

Mr Chivasa thought for a moment. 'It's partly because sex is involved. People are shy about their sex lives and don't want to do anything in public that indicates what they do in private.'

Nelson remembered something Viki had said. 'It would be good if *everyone* who came to the centre was given advice and was tested, not just those who were worried about being HIV positive. We could make this clear to the customers, then there'd be no reason for that shyness, would there? Everyone would be the same.'

Daniel was just behind them. He put in, 'You mean everyone who comes to the café at the centre – as a kind of condition of being allowed to use the centre?'

'No, no. Just if they want to, but make it kind of … fashionable, *the* thing to do,' Nelson said over his shoulder.

Mr Chivasa said, 'If they liked the centre enough, it might work. You could give them a free meal if they agreed to a test and a chat!'

They arrived at Nelson's truck and the two men shook hands again.

'*Best of luck, Nelson Mbizi,*' sang Daniel. '*But you know, it won't be easy!*' Nelson drove away with a smile.

# Chapter 13 *Business plan*

The next evening, Nelson left the hotel early to have time to go to the old garage and get measurements for his business plan. He'd had no further news from his parents. He'd also noticed he was being followed by a small black car, but he tried to act naturally anyway. Nothing he did was going to help anyone find his father.

Nelson drove up to the Chivasas' house when he'd finished and found that Daniel was just back from singing in the shopping mall.

'Have you got time to come with me to visit Sister Michael at the hospice?' Nelson asked him.

Daniel's face lit up. 'Oh yeah! *Gotta see my sis at the hospice, make sure Blessing's not been messing*, and give the Sister some money. Thanks, Nelson. There's no direct bus. Going in your truck would be great!'

They drove over to the hospice with Daniel singing all the way. He especially liked Kundai Kambera's songs, and Nelson had to ask him to sing something else when he'd sung the same one three times. Nelson also said he didn't need to pay for Blessing's care, but Daniel insisted he wanted to.

By the time they drove into the hospice yard it was dark. Nelson got out and said, 'Just a minute,' to Daniel. He wanted to check out the black car that was now parked outside the gate.

A white lady was walking towards the truck. Daniel held out his hand to her. 'You must be Sister Michael.'

'Indeed, I am. And I would say you're Lily Anne's big brother.' She smiled, shaking his hand.

Daniel towered over her. 'I'm Daniel. Our big brother is Eddy. I want to thank you, Sister Michael …'

'It's I who should be thanking you, Daniel. Lily Anne's a darling. She's forever looking for ways to help, reading to our guests, cleaning, cooking …'

'She kept our mother alive for much longer than we boys could have,' said Daniel.

'But nothing is going to keep little Blessing alive for long, you know.' The Sister's blue eyes were sympathetic.

'We all know that, Sister. It's just wonderful he can be in a place like this for the rest of his short life.' Daniel looked around in the dim light at the clean, neat yard.

'And where is Mr Nelson?' asked the Sister.

'He's being followed, so he's asking them who they are!' Daniel laughed.

'I'm not surprised. I read about his troubles. He must be very busy now, with his father away and all those hotels to run.'

'He needs to stay busy,' said Daniel, thinking of Viki.

'Worrying about his parents, is he?'

'Yes, yes, that's it,' agreed Daniel. 'He's got a lot to worry about suddenly.'

'And yet he still has time to think of the orphans and the sick. He's a gift from God, that's what he is.'

Daniel laughed. 'No more than you are, Sister!'

'Stop your nonsense, young Daniel. That's my job! Come and see the children.' And Sister Michael led Daniel into the children's building.

Nelson hadn't been able to communicate with the driver of the black car. The windows were black too, and the driver was pretending not to be there in the dark.

Nelson found the others inside. While Daniel and his brother and sister were playing together, he asked Sister Michael for a word outside.

'Sister, I need your advice,' he began.

'Whatever for, young Nelson?' asked Sister Michael.

'I've had an idea about how to help people in Sector D to learn about living with HIV in the community without being so afraid and secretive.' Nelson suddenly felt embarrassed. This was a woman of the church who would never have sex, never marry. How could he talk to her about these things?

'And what might that be?' she asked, gesturing for him to sit with her on a bench by the wall.

As Nelson told her all about his plans, and the business plan for the charity, he forgot about his embarrassment.

In the end she declared, 'That's amazing, young man. I'm proud of you! What can I do to help?'

'I shall need nurses and experienced advisors, a laboratory assistant, a visiting doctor, drugs. I need to know what those would cost and where to find them,' said Nelson. 'I want to open the centre before the rains come, so it's quite urgent.'

'I'll ask around,' promised Sister Michael. 'With the cuts in the Health Service budget, there are lots of nurses and advisors looking for work.' She looked serious. 'But the drugs may be a problem. They're just not available in this country any more. The Health Service doesn't have enough and HIV drugs are too expensive for most people to afford.'

'I may have to make a direct arrangement with a drugs company abroad, then.' Nelson had already thought of this, and was researching into how to do it.

'You'll need a qualified doctor,' said the Sister.

'Can you recommend anyone?'

'Indeed I can. He's a wonder. He comes to us almost every day and gets no more than a cup of tea as payment.'

'Could you let me have his number?'

'Of course,' said Sister Michael, standing up. 'Let's go to the office.'

As they walked across the yard, Sister Michael said quietly, 'Do you suppose the financial crisis in the Health Ministry has anything to do with the money they say your father stole?'

Nelson thought a moment. 'You mean, someone stole it from the Health Service budget, then tried to "borrow" from the Trade Ministry to replace the missing sum?'

'Maybe your father stood up to them and refused.'

'So,' said Nelson, 'they accused him of stealing the money so as not to be found out themselves.'

'It wouldn't be the first time in the history of human beings,' said Sister Michael with a sad smile.

\* \* \*

Nelson dropped Daniel off on his way home later. There was no news at home, and Philomena and Cook had both gone to the staff cottage. Nelson found it difficult to relax. He kept expecting the police to come back.

He gave up trying to sleep and went on with his business plan, but he couldn't help thinking about his father's problems too. He thought about trying to prove who had put his father in this position. It must be someone really high up in the government. That meant they'd be very powerful. Eventually he decided he was right not to have anything to do with politics.

*   *   *

Over the next few days, Nelson went to see the other two smaller hotels and got to know more of the staff. He read about his father's supposed crimes in the papers and the Intelligence Agency's guesses as to where Washington Mbizi was now. He tried calling his mother several times on her mobile, but she was always out of range.

When he'd finished his business plan, with help from Sister Michael and her doctor, he took it to his bank. They took a couple of days to approve it and passed it directly on to a lawyer. After two hours of detailed questions and answers and filling in forms, the lawyer told him it was a good plan, so Nelson prepared the final documents asking for money to start up a drop-in centre. If the charity in America said yes, his dream would be possible.

The day he sent the documents by email, Nelson felt a bit lost. That plan had kept him busy when he wasn't doing hotel work. Now he had nothing to do except wait – and try not to worry about his parents. As he was having dinner alone at home, Philomena told him there'd been a phone call from his mother that day.

'She just said she was fine and she'd call again,' Philomena said.

So Nelson called his mother's mobile, feeling relieved and pleased. But instead of hearing her voice, he heard a machine saying, 'This number is no longer in service.'

# Chapter 14 *Good news*

At the hotel two mornings later, there was a tall man with sunglasses waiting for Nelson. He wasn't the man from the police station. He asked to go somewhere private. Nelson felt a great stone settle in his stomach.

In Mr Mbizi's office the man asked Nelson, 'You heard from your father?'

'No, not for a few days,' answered Nelson. 'I'm getting really worried. He hasn't been away so long without being in touch before – and all that rubbish in the papers ...'

'He was in Johannesburg until yesterday,' the man said. 'But now we can't find him.'

Nelson was shocked. 'I ... haven't heard anything. I ... I haven't been able to contact either him or my mother.'

'I just thought you should know. We think the people he was working for – the ones he stole the money for – we think they've decided to get rid of him.'

'What are you saying?' asked Nelson, horrified.

'Don't know. Why don't you try to reach him?' The man went to the door. 'And don't try leaving the country yourself,' he said as he left.

Nelson tried to think. His father hadn't stolen any money for anyone, so there wasn't anyone wanting to get rid of him. The Intelligence Agency must have lost track of him, and now they wanted Nelson to try and call him so they could listen in. Or had they 'got rid of him' themselves and were trying to blame someone else?

With that thought, Nelson jumped up in panic just as he heard an email arrive on his laptop.

The charity had accepted his proposal! They had a couple more questions and wanted to send someone to see it when the centre was ready. But he should go ahead if he could afford to and the money would be available soon.

Nelson wanted to feel excited, but he was much too worried. He wrote a note to himself to contact the garage owner and agree to the rent.

While he was doing that, his mobile rang. It was a number he didn't recognise. 'Hello?' he said.

'Hello, Nelson,' said Ruby.

'Mum! Are you OK? They're saying here that Dad might be dead.' Nelson spoke quietly and shut the door.

'No, he's not dead.' She sounded very tense. 'He's just … travelling. I spoke to him just now.'

Nelson sat down suddenly in his father's chair. 'Phew! And are you OK? What's wrong with your phone?'

'I'm fine. We've changed our phones so they can't find us through the numbers. I'm staying here with my cousin.'

'Thank God for that,' said Nelson with relief.

'Your father said he'd try to find an international buyer for the Lion Hills – if you agree.' Ruby's voice broke. 'It … We won't be back for a while, and we'll need money.'

Nelson's heart sank. 'OK, Mum. I'll keep it all going till I hear from Dad. Do you want me to come and see you?'

'No. You stay there. I'm fine. We mustn't talk for long.'

'Tell Dad I'll do whatever he says about the hotel. Just ask him to let me know exactly what he wants.'

'Thanks, Nelson. I'll tell him if I can. I love you.'

'I love you too, Mum. Take real care.'

'Bye, Nelson.'

Nelson put his phone away. Perhaps he should change his number too. But for now he had too much to do to get the centre started. He picked up the desk phone.

* * *

Philomena was laying the table when Nelson got home that evening. 'Can you come with me to Sector D after dinner?' he asked. 'We've got the go-ahead for the centre. I want to talk to Mr Chivasa about it. I thought you might like to come too.'

Philomena laughed. 'Cook and I will make some sandwiches and biscuits while you eat,' she promised.

It turned into a big party at the Chivasas' house that evening. The youngest children had gone to bed, but they got up and joined in the fun as everyone chatted and sang. Mr Chivasa told Nelson he could organise getting the old garage clean in the afternoons, after he got back from his job. He'd employ some of the young men in the Sector who had no work. Mrs Chivasa said she'd find women to help too.

At about ten o'clock the neighbours came over to complain about the noise. But when they heard what was going on, they joined in and brought a radio. So the music went on well into the night.

* * *

During the next few days, Nelson organised with Fletcher to use some money from the business to open a bank account for the centre.

While Nelson worked long hours to prepare the Lion Hills Hotel for sale in case his father found a buyer, in Sector D Mr Chivasa employed a work party of young men to clean and paint the building, and clear the yard at the old garage. Eddy came over on his day off to lend a hand and Daniel helped too, when he wasn't at school or singing in the shopping mall.

And in the mall, the shoppers were getting to know Daniel. He'd started singing his own songs in between the ones he sang for the shop. Sometimes he did requests.

One afternoon he was asked for his song 'about the fat lady shopping'. He sang it in a high, desperate voice.

*Let me through. I gotta go home.*
*Can't you see, I need more room.*
*I bought the hat and I bought the suit.*
*I bought some shoes and I bought some boots.*
*I gotta get home 'cause my feet are dying,*
*Crying, trying to get home ...*

There were a lot of shouts and laughs as he sang.

When he finished, a loud voice called out, 'Can you stop for a minute? I want a word.'

Everyone turned round to see a man of about twenty-five in sunglasses and a big hat.

'Sure,' Daniel said to the stranger.

'What's your name?' asked the man.

'Who wants to know?' asked Daniel with a smile. The man was quite short, well-dressed and tough-looking.

He took off his sunglasses. Daniel stepped back. It was Kundai Kambera!

'I like what I hear,' said Kundai, without smiling.

'Oh, wow!' For once, Daniel had nothing to say.

'Yes, you're good. Could you do a few minutes in my show on Saturday? One of my singers ... died yesterday.' Kundai's eyes were wet. He put the sunglasses back on.

'Sure. Yeah. Of course! What do you want me to do?'

'Just sing two or three songs at the live concert,' said Kundai. 'Do you sing more serious ones?'

'Yes. Some of my songs are serious.'

'What about an instrument?'

'Well, I have an mbira, but I'm learning guitar.'

'Come to the Studio on 9th Street, number 115, tomorrow evening,' said Kundai. 'We'll be practising from about six. I'll lend you a guitar if you need one.'

'Right,' said Daniel, trying to sound businesslike.

Kundai said, 'Have five songs ready to choose from.'

'Thanks, Mr Kambera.'

'Thank *you*. Your song made me smile on a sad day.'

'See you tomorrow.' Daniel grinned.

Kundai Kambera walked away. Daniel saw two men, who had been looking in shop windows, join him as he left.

The people around Daniel broke into excited chatter. He couldn't stop smiling, so he sang the fat lady song again and the crowd laughed and clapped.

Later Daniel took a bus to the cemetery. He stood by his mother's grave and told her about his good luck. In the quiet sunset he sang a gentle song to her. He suddenly felt her near and heard her voice say, 'Your talent is a gift from God. Take care of it.' Tears ran down his smiling face. Stars were shining in the black sky when he left.

On his way home, Daniel stopped at the phone box in Sector D and called Phil, the cameraman. He told him about being in Kundai's live show on Saturday, and about Nelson's new drop-in centre. Phil said he'd see what his programme boss thought of the story. Daniel ran home. It had been a happy day.

# Chapter 15   *A day for sadness*

That Friday, Nelson had a message from his father. Washington Mbizi had called the lawyer, Mrs Murape, and she called Nelson. He was to expect a man called Paul Walker from Sydney, Australia, to arrive in Kurupenda the next day to discuss buying the Lion Hills Hotel. Mr Walker knew the hotel, as he'd stayed there on business in the past.

Nelson had planned to take the day off, but he spent the morning checking everything with Fletcher and the department managers, and making sure that they would be available the next day. After lunch he drove over to the old garage in Sector D.

When he got there, he couldn't believe the progress. The outside was now bright blue and the doors and windows were newly painted white. Red flowers on the great flamboyant tree were beginning to open. The ground around the building was clear and a row of chairs stood against the back wall, all different shapes and colours. The main door had a small tree on either side and was open, with a curtain to stop the flies. Loud music was coming from inside.

A large notice above the door said, 'THE GARAGE will repair your life.' Nelson laughed and pushed his way through the curtain. His dream really was coming true.

Daniel and Eddy were there with lots of other young people. A radio played on the clean, empty floor.

'Hey!' called Nelson.

'Nelson! Great to see you!' shouted Daniel.

'This is brilliant! Someone's been working hard!'

'Lots of someones!' said Eddy as he and Daniel came over to Nelson.

'But there's still a lot to do.' Daniel laughed. 'All the kitchen equipment, and the laboratory, and ...'

Kundai Kambera's voice on the radio suddenly filled the room with song. Eddy shouted to Nelson, 'Did you know Daniel's singing in Kundai's live show at the stadium tomorrow night? He met him at the shopping mall.'

'Hey! Congratulations!' said Nelson. 'That's fantastic! Are you going to be another Kundai then, Daniel?

'Sure,' replied Daniel over the music. 'He's from an even poorer place than Sector D. And now look at him!'

'Darling of the radio stations, a thousand girls running after him,' shouted Nelson. 'Not quite you, somehow.'

'A hundred girls would be enough for me,' answered Daniel. 'At least to start with!' They laughed so much they didn't hear Primrose come in.

'Hey, guys!' she called. She looked very serious.

'Hi, Mrs Chivasa,' said Daniel, turning the radio down.

'Mr Chivasa just had a call on his work mobile. I'm sorry, Daniel, Eddy, but ... It was Sister Michael to say that Blessing has died.' The boys put their arms around each other and hid their faces. 'She says they'll bury him tomorrow morning at the hospice unless you want him buried with his mother. Please call her back.'

After a few seconds, Eddy looked up. 'Thank you, Mrs Chivasa,' he said.

Daniel wiped tears off his face and said, 'We'd better get over there.'

'I'll take you,' said Nelson.

On the way, Daniel suddenly remembered something.

'I'd better call Phil later and tell him not to bother trying to come,' he said.

Nelson's hand on the steering wheel shook, but he kept his voice calm as he said, 'Did he say they'd come to the show tomorrow?'

'He said they might. But I'm not sure if I'll be able to do the show now. It doesn't seem right with little Blessing …' There were tears on Daniel's cheeks.

Nelson put a hand on his arm. 'I think you'll find that Kundai will expect you to sing as promised. But call Phil now, if you want.' Nelson got his mobile out of his pocket.

Daniel sighed. 'Well, even so, I don't really want the TV people around,' he said as he pressed the numbers.

'Yebo?' Phil answered his phone.

'Phil? This is Daniel Mawadza.'

'Hi, Daniel. What's up?'

'Phil, my little brother just died, so I don't think it's a good idea to come tomorrow, after all.'

'I'm with Viki. She was saying we might make it. Hang on. I'll just tell her.' There was a pause. Suddenly Daniel was listening to Viki's voice.

'Hey, Daniel. Sorry to hear about little Blessing. Are you going to have a funeral?'

'We're going to bury him with my mum and we hope Sister Michael will come and say some words. Why?'

'That would make great TV, so we'll be there …'

'But …'

'And you're in Kundai Kambera's live show, aren't you? Tomorrow night at the football stadium?'

'Yes, but I ... You could ... In ten days or so Nelson's drop-in centre opens. That would be more interesting.'

'Not so, Daniel. Babies dying are better television. The viewers like to hear about bad luck. Makes them feel good about their own lives.'

Daniel felt sick. 'Do what you want,' he said and pressed the red button. 'I'm not so sure about her any more,' he said as he handed the phone back to Nelson.

'Who do you mean?' Nelson asked.

'That was Viki. They're coming tomorrow to film the funeral. She says bad luck stories make good TV.'

'Pretty sad, huh?' said Eddy.

Daniel went on, 'I met someone when I was practising at the studio with Kundai. This girl used to know Viki at school. She said Viki was not always so ... so ...'

'So nasty?' Nelson asked.

'I was thinking of a different word,' said Daniel. 'I know it's probably just anger, but it's eating her up.'

'We're all pretty angry these days,' said Eddy. 'I'm still angry about Mum. I have to run up and down the street sometimes, so I don't lose my temper. How do you feel about what's happening to your dad, Nelson?'

'Usually I'm too busy to think about how I feel these days.' Nelson was quiet for a few moments. Then he went on, 'I learned a long time ago not to let anger stop me thinking, at least not for long. My dad did a lot of things that made me angry, and if I showed it, he just locked me up or hit me ... or both.'

'Well, today is for sadness, not anger,' said Daniel, and they drove on in silence.

# Chapter 16   *Goodbye, Blessing*

Everyone was at the cemetery very early next day. The sun made long shadows of the few tired trees and the silent crowd round Melanie Mawadza's grave. Only Nelson was missing as he had to meet the Australian at the airport. Daniel noticed Viki and Phil arrive. He couldn't believe they were really so heartless.

He walked over to them and, looking down at Viki, said, 'Do not say a word, or move anyone or anything around. I don't want to know you're here.'

Viki looked surprised at his anger and said, 'OK, Daniel. Just a fly on the wall, as we say.'

'Right,' said Daniel. He nodded to Phil, who nodded back sympathetically, and returned to the graveside.

Sister Michael was saying, 'Blessing died with a smile on his face. He knew he would be with his mother soon.'

Daniel found he couldn't stop his tears enough to sing, so little Blessing was gently lowered into the earth on top of his mother in silence. Then Philomena and other friends began the loud traditional weeping.

Suddenly Lily Anne fell to the ground. Eddy and Daniel both put an arm round her. Sister Michael came over.

'Eddy, can you come back to the hospice with Lily Anne? We need to do some paperwork, and you're the man of the family.'

'Come on, Lily Anne,' said Eddy. 'You've grown too much for me to carry you.' He walked her slowly towards the hospice truck.

Sister Michael turned to Daniel. 'Get back home now, Daniel,' she said kindly. 'You'll need your strength for tonight. You can cry for Blessing tomorrow, if you must, but you know he's better where he is.'

'Thank you, Sister. I'll be OK in a minute.'

'Right then. Good luck tonight!'

As the truck drove away, Daniel turned and saw Viki and Phil. They were arguing about something, as usual.

He walked over to them, his anger suddenly sharp as a knife.

'So. Are you happy now?' he said directly to Viki.

'What do you mean?' asked Viki.

'Got your pictures of the dead baby going home to his dead mother, and his brothers and sister crying, did you?'

'Yes. We did. We got exactly that.' Viki's eyes flashed.

But Daniel couldn't stop. 'Well, isn't that nice? Now all your viewers can see how death tidies up after AIDS. They can think how lucky they've been that they haven't lost their whole family yet. They can think how lucky I am that I still have a brother and a sister. But then, perhaps you haven't thought that some of them may be in a worse situation than I am ...'

'I doubt it.' Viki was standing as tall as she could. 'Most of the people who watch my stuff aren't from places like Sector D where there's nowhere they can go for help. Some of the people who see these programmes have plenty of time and money. So that's what I'm saying in my pieces – that things are really, really bad, and they must do something.'

'And yet when you meet someone who really *is* doing something, you can't even be polite!' Daniel was trying not to shout in this holy place, but all his fear and sadness were pouring out as anger.

'I suppose you mean Nelson. I suppose he's been telling you that I was a bit cold to him. Well, he was trying to be romantic and it was stupid.'

'And that's not allowed with a professional woman like you, of course. A woman who uses other people's bad luck to move up in her career, to make herself a TV star.'

Viki gasped. 'Is that what you think I'm doing?'

'I don't think,' shouted Daniel, 'I know! I see you making money out of the deaths of babies, out of the grief of orphans and grandmothers, and it turns my stomach.'

Viki's eyes suddenly filled with tears. 'You have no idea what you're saying,' she said. 'I ... I don't believe ... you can believe ...'

She turned away ... and walked straight into a tree she hadn't seen behind her. She dropped her notebook and sat down slowly on the earth at the foot of the tree. She hid her face in her hands and made strange, hard sounds. Her whole body shook and tears bled through her fingers.

Daniel stood staring in horror. He looked round for Phil, but he had already gone to their truck out on the main road.

Daniel walked quickly away from the tree. Then he walked back again. Viki was still on the ground. He walked away again, and stood beside another new grave. There were plastic flowers, white against the red earth, lying on it. He took a deep breath and remembered what Nelson had said about not letting his anger stop him from thinking.

He turned and looked at Viki again. She was wiping her face on her blouse. She looked up and saw him still there. She stood up quickly and looked around for her notebook.

Daniel walked over and picked it up from behind the tree. As he gave it to her, she whispered, 'Thank you.'

He walked beside her in silence towards the road. 'You're wrong about me, you know,' she said at last.

'Perhaps I am,' said Daniel. 'And anyway it doesn't matter what a sixteen-year-old schoolboy thinks of you. But it does matter what other people say about you, and I don't like to see you making people hate you. You can be kind, I've seen it.'

They stopped beside the truck. 'Do they hate me? Actually hate me?'

'Well, you're not exactly lovable most of the time.'

'Nor is this world.' There was anger in her eyes again.

'You may think so, and perhaps you're right … but I usually find it rather wonderful,' said Daniel.

'You're … different,' she said, with a small smile.

'No. We're all born the same. We just become different and forget about the sameness.'

'That's what I mean. You think differently!' Her smile grew. She really was beautiful when her eyes weren't burning. Daniel wanted Nelson to see her like this.

'Where are you going now?' he asked.

'We're going to try and get an interview with Kundai before his show.'

'Why don't you come over to the Garage,' he suggested, 'and see how it's getting on?'

'I'm hungry now,' she smiled, 'after all those tears. Do you want to come with us and get a sandwich on the way? Or is someone taking you back?'

'Will Phil look after me if you go back to being angry?' asked Daniel, making a little-boy face.

'Will he protect me if *you* get angry again?' Viki almost laughed.

Phil looked confused, but smiled and said, 'I'll sit in the middle.' Which made them all laugh.

At the sandwich bar they got sandwiches and bottles of water. They took them outside, sat on the wall in the shade and ate in silence. Then, as they were collecting up their rubbish to put in the bin, Viki went round the other side of the truck. Daniel could see her through the windows. She got some pills out of her bag and took them with some water from her bottle.

Daniel went round the truck and stood behind her. 'How often do you take those?' he asked.

She jumped and then turned to look up at him. 'Oh, just when I have a headache,' she said with a smile.

'You're lying,' he said sadly. 'You take them three times a day, with food, don't you?'

'None of your business,' said Viki, looking him straight in the eyes. 'Keep out of my life, Daniel.'

'I'm in your life for a reason. And you're in my life for a reason.'

'No, Daniel. Life isn't like that.'

'It is … if you want it to be.'

She turned away and got into the truck. 'We'll go to the Garage,' she said. So Phil drove them to Sector D.

# Chapter 17   *Meeting at the Garage*

As they drove, Daniel's thoughts raced. 'What must it be like for Viki? No wonder she keeps people away from her. And how am I going to tell Nelson?'

Meanwhile, he was directing them to the Garage. When they got there, Viki gasped. It looked wonderful.

The sun was shining on the newly cleaned roof. There was a line of teenagers planting something along the back fence. They were singing a Kundai song about 'Love in the time of AIDS'. There was different music coming out of the main door and a couple of girls were sitting in the shade counting tiny packets of biscuits from one box to another.

Phil parked the truck under the big tree in the back yard. 'Amazing ...' he said to Daniel, with a big smile.

'This might work!' said Viki, as she got out. She walked off round the side of the building to explore further.

Daniel couldn't see Nelson's truck, but he knew Nelson would be on his way to the Garage with Sister Michael and her nurse. They had an appointment to meet the man who was going to furnish the clinic. Phil walked away with his camera, and Viki wasn't in sight.

Daniel heard Nelson's truck coming and stood ready to open his door. Sister Michael and the nurse got out the other side.

'I need to tell you something very important,' Daniel said in Nelson's ear.

'Go ahead,' said Nelson.

'Not here. It's … well, it seems to be a secret …'

'Right.' Nelson took the two women through the back door into what was going to be the laboratory and advice rooms, and left them to have a look around.

Daniel sat on one of the chairs outside by the wall. When Nelson came out, they both sat and watched the line of teenagers in front of them across the yard.

Daniel took a breath. 'I saw Viki taking ARVs,' he said.

Nelson sat motionless and silent.

'We had a sandwich together this morning,' Daniel went on. 'She took some pills afterwards. She didn't want us to see her and she said it was none of my business when I asked about them. But I'm sure that's what they were.'

'So she's HIV positive,' said Nelson. 'That explains a lot.'

They sat listening to the teenagers singing for a while. The two girls counting packets of biscuits finished, stood up, and took their boxes inside.

'Did Viki come to the funeral?' Nelson asked.

'Yeah, she did.' Daniel was embarrassed. 'I was … I lost my temper with her afterwards. I told her she was using the deaths of babies to make herself into a TV star.'

'My God!'

'She cried, but she did seem to see why I was hurt.'

'She did?' Nelson hardly dared believe Viki could feel for others. 'You must have made quite an impression …'

Daniel jumped up. 'I just remembered. The funeral was too much for Lily Anne. I must ask Sister Michael how she is!' He went in.

Nelson didn't move. He shut his eyes and felt tears run down his face. His heart felt as though it was being pressed between two stones.

'What's the matter?' said a gentle voice.

Nelson opened his eyes. The gentle voice was Viki's! She sat down beside him. He sat forward, hesitated, and then took her hand. She didn't pull it away.

'You're HIV positive,' he said.

'You guessed.' She was looking at their hands.

'Daniel told me about the ARVs.'

After a moment Viki said, 'The man I went with knew he was positive, but he didn't tell me.'

'Have *you* told *him*?'

'I nearly killed him.'

'But you're still angry,' Nelson stated.

'I wanted to get married, have kids. He's stolen all that.' Viki's mouth was a hard line. She stared at the fence.

'So you wouldn't let anyone near you ...'

'What's the use? I can't give a man love and children without killing him.'

'There are ways ...' Nelson couldn't meet her eyes.

'No man wants to bother ...'

'Depends on how much he loves you.' He turned and looked at her.

She didn't answer, her eyes still on the fence.

'So what are you going to do?' he asked.

She turned to him. 'What *can* I do? My job ...' She paused.

'... and trying to make sure people know how to stop themselves getting sick,' Nelson added.

'Yes. Like I said at dinner that night.'

'I should have guessed ...' Nelson said. 'Sorry.'

'I'm glad you didn't, but I'm sorry too. I was very ... rude.' The faintest smile touched her lips.

'So was I,' Nelson smiled, 'when I left you at the hotel!'

'That was ... I suppose I deserved that. But, you see ... It's just ... I'm just so ... Well ...' Viki looked down at her hand in Nelson's. 'So frightened, to tell you the truth.'

'That's why I was crying just now,' said Nelson.

'Sorry?'

'Because I was imagining what it would be like,' Nelson said very softly, 'to be alone and know you were positive.'

Viki suddenly held Nelson's hand very tight.

He stood up and pulled her to her feet. He put his arms around her and said, 'But you don't have to be alone.' She pushed her face into his chest to hide her tears. They stood still, holding each other in the sunlight.

Daniel came out of the door, saw them, and went straight back in, with a huge grin.

At last Viki took a deep breath and stood back from Nelson, wiping her eyes. All around them stood a silent circle of watchers, Daniel and the nurse and Sister Michael among them. When Viki smiled they all began to clap.

'So you'll be wanting to get on and finish this film you're making,' said Sister Michael.

'Yes. Of course.' Viki laughed. 'Where's Phil?'

'He's having a cool drink over by the river,' said Sister Michael.

Nelson forced himself to come back to earth and looked at his watch. 'I've got to go and meet this businessman from Australia now. I left him to freshen up. I'm hoping he's going to buy the Lion Hills Hotel,' he explained. 'Daniel, shall I take you into town? Do you need to practise for tonight?'

'I wanted to see Lily Anne ...' Daniel began.

'She's sleeping, Daniel. She's fine, just very, very tired and sad,' said Sister Michael. 'I'll try and bring her to the show this evening.'

'Then, yes, I'd better get some practice!'

'The show starts at eight,' said Nelson. 'Let's all meet up at the football stadium, at seven thirty.'

'Kundai said I'd be given eight tickets, so I'll meet you at Gate H, and give them to you.' Daniel suddenly couldn't stand still. He understood how important this evening was going to be, how important this whole day was. He found it hard not to start singing now. 'I'll see you at the truck in five minutes,' he said to Nelson and ran off to the Chivasa house to get his mbira.

Nelson left Daniel at the football stadium. They could hear music and tests being made on the sound equipment. Daniel ran in with a quick word of thanks.

Nelson took a few minutes to consider what had happened with Viki. He was so excited and happy he could hardly think. If she wanted to be with him as much as he wanted to be with her, there'd be problems because they lived and worked so far apart. And there'd be problems eventually because of her HIV status, though he knew there were solutions. But for now he only wanted to remember how it felt to hold and comfort her. He'd nearly fainted with happiness.

'Well, I'd better go and sell a hotel.' He laughed to himself. 'Then I'll have more time to be with her.'

# Chapter 18   *The show*

'Nelson!' shouted the big, soft Australian called Paul Walker. He was sitting in an armchair near reception at the hotel and had to work hard to stand up from it.

'Hello, Mr Walker,' said Nelson. 'Please come this way to my office.'

They went up in the lift to Washington Mbizi's top-floor office. There, Paul Walker looked hard at Nelson.

'You heard from your father about this deal?' he asked.

Nelson was surprised. 'Only from our lawyer.'

Paul gave Nelson a sealed envelope. 'You might want to read this before we get down to business.'

Nelson opened the envelope and found a note to him in his father's handwriting.

*I've discussed the deal for the Lion Hills with Paul Walker. He's agreed on a price I think is good, but you should check that he doesn't want either of the other hotels. If he does, make sure he pays for it! Tell your mother I'm fine. Dad.*

The note was dated three days before.

'How did you get this?' Nelson asked Paul.

'Saw the man himself.'

'What?!'

'Yeah. He was in our part of the world last week. Looked well. He's moved on already, so I don't know where he is now. What does he say about the deal?'

Nelson put the note in his pocket. He'd get on the phone to his mother and confirm that his father was fine in a few minutes, but first he said, 'Come and see round the hotel. When you've seen it, we can discuss the price ...'

They went all over the hotel and then sat down with Fletcher and the hotel manager and the account books.

In the end, Paul was happy and they agreed a price, but Nelson wanted to make sure all the employees would be kept on. Paul couldn't promise that, but he said he'd discuss it with the lawyers at the next stage of the sale.

\* \* \*

Viki and Phil got to Gate H at the football stadium before any of the others, but there were already thousands of fans arriving for the show. Viki was happy with the work she and Phil had done at the Garage and the hospice.

'You're staying on for a couple of days then?' Phil asked.

Viki raised an eyebrow at him.

'Seems to me,' he said, 'you might have things to talk to Nelson about.'

'Maybe ... He hasn't said anything – and I'm not sure how I'm feeling at the moment.'

'Well, from long experience of working with you, I'd say you look about the best I've ever seen you,' said Phil, his face completely serious.

'Oh, Phil!' Viki laughed.

'See? Third time you've laughed today.'

'OK. If Nelson isn't too busy and wants me to, I'll stay on and come back on Monday. We have two stories to cover in Durban on Tuesday, haven't we?'

'Yup.'

Daniel appeared at a run. 'Tickets!' he said and pushed them into Viki's hand. 'See you.' And he was gone.

'Good luck,' Phil called after him. 'Look, Viki, they've said I can film Daniel, but from the platform with the other cameramen, so I'll have to go and get organised.'

'Fine. Go ahead. I'll wait for everyone. Is there a break in the show?'

'Yeah. Just before Kundai comes on,' Phil said.

'Can we do a "speaking to the camera" piece then?'

'Sure, but you'll have to come to me,' he warned. 'It's that big platform thing in the middle.'

'I'll come there as soon as Daniel's finished.'

'Right. See you.' And Phil left her just as Nelson appeared with Sister Michael, Lily Anne, Eddy and Philomena.

'Hi, Viki. Do we have tickets?' asked Nelson, suddenly filled with delight at seeing her.

'Hi. Here they are,' she said, unable to meet his eyes. They found their seats and Viki sat at the end of the row so she could get out to meet Phil. Nelson sat beside her.

'How did your meeting go?' she asked him. They both sat, their hands between their knees, looking at the stage.

'The Australian has agreed a price for the Lion Hills Hotel. He may even consider the other two hotels …'

'But once it goes through, you'll be free to work full time for the Garage?' Viki asked.

'Well, not if I still have the two smaller hotels to run, but freer than now. Will Network 10 send you up again for the opening of the Garage in a couple of weeks?'

'I'm not sure.' Viki closed her eyes and sighed.

Nelson was looking at Viki's profile. He thought she looked too perfect to be true and he felt as though he owned the world. 'And I wanted to ask you something else.'

Viki turned to him. 'Oh?'

'May I come down to Jo'burg and spend a little time with you when things are a bit quieter here?' asked Nelson.

'Do you really want to?'

'Not really. I'm just <u>making conversation to kill time</u>,' Nelson joked.

'Oh!' Viki's laughter died quickly. 'Look. Truly. Part of me wants to see you more than you can imagine and ...'

'I doubt it ...' said Nelson.

'... part of me knows it's stupid. There's no future ...' Viki went on.

'But there *is* a present. Surely we can enjoy that?' said Nelson.

Viki smiled more happily. 'OK. Let's just enjoy the present.' She held out her hand to him. He took it in both his and kissed it.

They sat in silence waiting for the show to start.

Two or three singers came and went on the stage, introduced by a man with a microphone. People clapped, but they weren't really interested. They'd come to see Kundai and he wasn't on until after the break. The crowd chatted and moved around.

The man with the microphone came on and said, 'Until a month ago, the next place on the programme was filled by Orlando. You may know that Orlando died a few days ago. We miss him and thank him for his wonderful music.' The crowd went quiet and there was a short pause.

'But now,' said the man, 'we're going to hear from Daniel Mawadza. You may have seen and heard him singing in the 7th Street Shopping Mall. Here he is, at the special invitation of Kundai. Give him a big hand.'

Eddy stood up and called out, 'Go for it, Dan!' Others clapped and whistled. Lily Anne just stood up and waited.

'Good evening, everyone,' came Daniel's voice over the microphone. He was wearing jeans he had borrowed from Nelson and a plain white T-shirt. He was carrying a borrowed guitar and his mbira. He came forward and sat on a small wooden seat he brought with him.

'That was our dad's,' said Eddy quietly.

Daniel laid the guitar down beside him, sat down with his mbira and said, 'I'll start with a quick trip along 7th Street with one of my favourite ladies.' People laughed and clapped.

His next song was the one about his mother dying. The whole football ground went quiet. Some people remembered seeing Daniel on TV. They clapped for a long time at the end of the song.

'And now, I have a new song. It's called "Sometimes you know, but you don't want to know"'. Daniel stood up, picked up the guitar and played louder, happier music.

*Sometimes you know, but you don't want to know.*
*The truth's too sharp, too heavy, too near.*
*But you gotta listen so you can hear*
*Your heart saying, love's allowed.*
*Love's allowed. Just don't hate us.*
*Love's allowed, whatever your status.*
*Even when you know, but you don't want to know …*

As Daniel finished, the crowd clapped and called out, and those who were standing in the middle of the football field were jumping up and down.

Then the man with the microphone shouted, 'Thank you Daniel. Now we'll take a break and … in fifteen minutes … the great, the brilliant, Kundai Kambera will be here!'

The crowd cheered wildly as the lights came up.

'I have to meet Phil down at the platform,' said Viki to Nelson. She had tears on her face, but she was laughing. 'Wasn't Daniel amazing? Lily Anne, Eddy, do you want to come and talk to me on camera about him?'

'Yeah!' they shouted and followed her into the crowd.

Nelson turned to Sister Michael. 'He really is good,' he said. 'How does he know all that stuff about how people feel?'

'He watches. And of course he feels too. Did I hear you telling Viki that the hotel deal is going through?'

'Almost certainly, yes.'

'So how do you feel about that?'

'Happy that it will mean I'm freer. Sad to say goodbye to the hotel ...'

'Well, by that smile on your face, I'd say the happy wins over the sad.' Sister Michael's blue eyes were laughing.

'Yeah, well ... That's partly because I learned that my dad's fine.' Philomena, at the other end of their row, gasped, and hugged her Sunday handbag.

'That's just perfect. Did you tell your mum?'

'First moment I had alone.'

'What else is making you smile then, young Nelson? Partly for your dad, and partly for what?'

'Partly because of Viki,' he said.

Sister Michael became serious. 'She's HIV positive, isn't she?'

'She told you?' asked Nelson in surprise.

'She did. And it'll be hard for you, you know.'

'Not as hard as living without her,' declared Nelson.

'Which in the end you might have to do.'

'Well, by then, with any luck, we'll have lots of happy memories – and even a child or two.'

'And so when will that happen, do you suppose?' Sister Michael was making fun of him. Philomena was pretending not to hear, smiling broadly at her handbag.

'Oh, probably tomorrow or the next day.' Nelson laughed. 'Unless of course she decides against it.'

'You know she won't … Look, here are the others coming back again. Will I see you soon at the hospice? We all have to decide what Lily Anne will do next.'

'Of course.'

Everyone sat down again and prepared to watch Kundai. The crowd was already singing his latest hit song. Viki took hold of Nelson's hand in the dark. 'Did Daniel know how you felt before you did?' she whispered.

'No, but he knew how *you* felt before *you* did!' Nelson whispered back.

She took his face between her hands and said, 'You just be glad he did!' And she kissed him.

# Epilogue

A year later Nelson and Viki's son, Daniel, was born. 'Big' Daniel was still at school, but had made a CD in London and done a tour of concerts with Kundai. Lily Anne had gone back to school. She spent a lot of time at the Garage with children and teenagers from families affected by HIV. Eddy was a bus driver when there was work, but also drove for Nelson. The Garage and the hospice often worked together. Money came in from other countries and organisations, partly because of films Viki made about their work. Viki's doctor said she might live an almost normal life for many years if she looked after herself and went on with the drugs. Little Daniel was given the drug that stopped him getting HIV from Viki, and it worked.

Ruby joined Washington Mbizi and they moved from country to country, waiting for a change in government in Gomokure.

\* \* \*

According to reports by the United Nations and the World Health Organisation, the average number of people living with HIV in most countries of Southern Africa rose to between one in five and one in four in 2005. In some places the figures can be as high as one in two. And the numbers are still rising for people between the ages of fifteen and forty-nine. In the same year there were more than four million children orphaned by AIDS in southern and central Africa.